THE CHURCH:
A Biblical Perspective

by

L.A. Stauffer

ISBN 1-58427-144-2

Guardian of Truth Foundation
P.O. Box 9670
Bowling Green, Kentucky 42102
1-800-428-0121

Table of Contents

Introduction

It is my privilege to introduce this book to its readers, and to introduce its author. Brother Stauffer is a very mature student and scholar in all things relating to the Bible. Most faithful brethren know him and know of his great ability, his scholarship and his experience in preaching and defending truth. Highly knowledgeable in the original Greek language, he has unique ability to "Preach the Word" in a clear and forceful manner that reaches the hearers everywhere.

This book is devoted to a vital study of the very church for which Christ died. It reaches into some of the important, yes, essential matters that it seems are being overlooked in the last two or three decades. We may have assumed that these matters are "settled" and that there is no urgency in this matter. If we continue in this way for another decade, we may have deprived the children and grand-children of fortification against the inroads of apostasy.

Brother Stauffer's discussion of early departures — of Catholicism and Protestantism — and his extensive clarification of the word *ekklēsia* very plainly introduce the nature of the church in its different uses in the New Testament. In other lessons we are warned of Calvinism and of Protestantism of every kind as well as present (and recent) departures in the body of Christ.

Brethren almost everywhere are being involved in gospel work in many "new" fields — those fields that have, for so many decades, been forbidden ground for the sowing of the good seed. This is a great and worthy — even necessary work for all of us. But while we become so enthused about such work we must also remember that we have done no service to Christ if we do not instill in the converts everywhere the facts and principles regarding the church. In many places it may be easier to convert souls than it is to help them know what the church really is, how it functions, etc.

Brother Stauffer's book will help, especially those who have not studied these matters for a while or others who have not heard this kind of message at all. I congratulate the writer of the book, and I commend "The Church: A Biblical Perspective" for serious study for all sincere seekers for truth.

— **Leslie Diestelkamp**

Restoration:
Speak As the Oracles of God

Introduction

Churches of today manifest an evolution of nearly twenty centuries of change. They often exhibit little resemblance to the creative design of the church Jesus built in the first century. Begotten by theologies and traditions of men, modern religious bodies reveal more about the thinking, the hopes, and the desires of their forefathers than of the Lord they claim to serve. For example:

- The mysteries of a ritualistic mass performed by a priestly-robed celebrant amidst symbols and forms of mystical and medieval art bears the image of an ancient, therefore authentic, religion. But is it of Christ (see John 4:24; 1 Cor. 11:23-25; Matt. 15:8,9)?

- Devotion to social and political reform as direct objectives of the church in a fight against crime, poverty, judicial inequities, prejudicial laws, etc. displays a commitment to love, the chief of God's commandments. But, were these the goals of the Lord's church (see Eph. 6:5-9; Col. 3:22-4:1; 1 Pet. 2:13-17)?

- Expanding the mission of the church to include recreational activities has shaped many religious bodies into the likeness of country clubs and reflects their desire to minister to the whole man. But, does this mirror the image of the church Jesus built (see Mark 16:15,16; Eph. 4:11-16)?

- Staged performances of professional choirs, entertaining gimmicks to draw crowds, and confusion and shouting and clapping by enthusiastic worshipers are rationalized as legitimate activities for the modern church. But, did the Lord or men author these practices (Matt. 21:23-25; 1 Cor. 14:26-33,40; John 6:26,27)?

- Modernistic theologians deny the personal nature of God, repudiate the bodily resurrection of Jesus, reject the verbal inspiration of Scripture, and seek compromise on the morality of homosexuality, the submissive role of women, the uniqueness of Christianity as a religion from God, and many other issues. But, does such broadmindedness grow out of the teaching of Jesus as taught in the Bible (Gen. 1:1; Luke 24:1-6; 1 Cor. 2:10-13; 2 Tim. 3:16,17; Rom. 1:26,27; 1 Tim. 2:12-15; John 14:6)?

Only a thorough search of the New Testament will answer questions about the original practices of the first-century church and the legitimacy of any of today's religious observances. But before that, it is important to look briefly at what transpired historically after the founding of the Lord's church. How did modern churches arrive at their present state?

Shortly after the apostles established churches of Christ in the first century they warned of an upcoming apostasy. Seducing spirits, lies, hypocrisy, and perverse teaching would in later times draw away disciples from the Lord, scatter the flock, and cause some to fall from the faith.

> But the spirit saith expressly, that in later times some shall fall away from the faith, giving heed to seducing spirits and doctrines of demons, through the hypocrisy of men that speak lies, branded in their own conscience as with a hot iron; forbidding to marry and commanding to abstain from meats (1 Tim. 4:1-3).
>
> I know that after my departing grievous wolves shall enter among you, not sparing the flock; and from among your own selves shall men arise, speaking perverse things, to draw away the disciples after them (Acts 20:29,30).

Apostasy: The Rise of Catholicism

Bishop over Elders. The second century had hardly begun when signs of the anticipated departures manifested themselves. Ignatius, in letters that date from A.D. 110-117, wrote glowingly of the elevation of one elder above others (*A History of Christianity*, Ray Petry 9-11). The exalted elder was distinguished as "the bishop," a decisive change from the original practice of a plurality of elders in every church — all known as bishops (Acts 14:23; 20:17,28; 1 Pet. 5:1-3). By A.D. 150 these "monarchical bishops had become well-nigh universal" (*The History of the Christian Church*, Williston Walker 48).

From that time the power of bishops was expanded to "metropolitan bishops" over major cities with many churches and "patriarchal bishops" over provincial areas. Next, synods and councils of bishops met to formulate creeds, issue orders, and replace the apostolic authority of the Scriptures. By the sixth and seventh centuries the bishop of Rome became "pope" or "universal father" of what became the Roman Catholic Church. Centuries of debate bolstered the preeminence of "papal authority" and the pope extended his powers, claimed infallibility, and became spokesman and head of the apostate body.

Hierarchy of Priests. Alongside the authoritative role of bishops developed the hierarchical and mystical powers of a special priesthood. The bishops and those they ordained functioned as intermediaries between God and man. They alone, it was claimed, could invoke the blessings of grace and channel them through sacraments to communicants. Priests, at first, asserted this power most prominently in the celebration of what was called "the mass."

By mid-second century Justin Martyr wrote of a mystical union of the body of Christ with the bread of the Lord's supper and the blood of Christ with the fruit of the vine (*A Handbook of the History of Christianity*, Ed. Tim Dowley 127). The special priesthood was well established by A.D. 300 and in time the sacramental mass was generally accepted. The "hierarch," the priest, petitioned the Spirit of God to transubstantiate the bread and the wine into the body and blood of Jesus and reoffered it as an "unbloody" sacrifice for the people. His priestly powers alone, it was believed, could transform these elements and convey the grace of God to the souls of the worshipers. This departure prepared Catholicism for the entire sacramental system, which was fine tuned and systematized by the days of Thomas Aquinas (1227-1274).

Sacramental System. Seven sacraments control members of the Catholic Church from birth till death. At birth the blessing of forgiveness allegedly flows through the sacrament of *baptism* and at death through *extreme unction*. In between, it is supposed, that strength for faithfulness comes through *confirmation*, forgiveness by auricular confession in *penance*, benefits of Christ's sacrifice in the *eucharist* (mass), and blessings of love for family life in *marriage*. All of this, they contend, is available only through a hierarchy of Priests ordained by bishops in *holy orders*.

The church, meaning the hierarchy of bishops and priests headed by the pope, stands directly between man and God. No access to grace or to God the Father, according to this system, is possible except by the church through the priesthood. Accepting the infallibility of the church, as it speaks through the pope, and affirming the dogma of doctrinal development, Catholicism continually initiates new doctrines and expands old ones.

Other Departures. The change of baptism from "immersion" to "sprinkling" and from a willing act of adults to an imposed act upon innocent infants is one clear example. The worship of Mary as the "mother of God" and as a "mediatrix" between God and man, prayers offered to designated saints with an assumed superabundance of merit, superstitious devotion to relics, crosses, crucifixes, and other so-called sacred objects are just a few of the new doctrines developed under the speculative eye of the "infallible" church.

Beyond fundamental doctrinal changes evolved a corrupt priesthood and clerical system. Priests harbored concubines, the church sold offices of bishops to the highest bidders, popes and bishops appointed favorite relatives to important positions, and the sacramental system reaped rewards of avarice, especially through penance and the sale of indulgences. The enlightened age of the Renaissance and Reformation could handle no more. Revolt and rebellions began.

Reformation: The Rise of Denominationalism

Indulgences. Martin Luther (1485-1546), a monk and young priest, abhorred the immorality he saw, but was more deeply disturbed by a system of theology that bore no resemblance to the teaching of the Bible from which, as a priest, he had lectured for several years. He saw specifically the lack of Bible authority for the pope's claims in general and the sale of indulgences in particular. In A.D. 1517 he rebelled against doctrinal corruption. His revolt began that year when John Tetzel came to Wittenberg, Germany, where Luther was lecturing. Tetzel was raising money to rebuild St. Peter's Cathedral in Rome by the sale of indulgences. Drawing on a supposed treasury of meritorious works stored up by saints, priests in penance granted indulgences: relief from the purging fires of purgatory. Indulgences could be obtained for oneself, a relative, or a loved one. In Luther's day indulgences had become certificates of forgiveness of sins that could be purchased with money.

95 Theses. Luther detected in the sacrament of penance and the sale of indulgences a scheme of buying or earning salvation. That, he knew from his biblical studies, was false. He, as a result, penned 95 theses or objections to the practice, nailed them to the door of the castle church in Wittenberg, and challenged all proponents to debate the issue. Luther based his criticisms on both reason and Scripture. This was a bold stroke. The young priest was saying that man by reason can understand the Scriptures and that the Scriptures determine right and wrong. He in his opposition to the sacrament of penance renounced the authority of the pope. From this he never wavered.

Pillars of the Movement. Luther's conclusions formed the basis of a new theology. Luther observed that the Bible, not the pope, is the sole authority in religious matters (see 2 Tim. 3:16,17; Gal. 1:8,9; 2 John 9). Every Christian, he also learned, is a priest and has direct access to God the Father through Jesus Christ (see Eph. 2:13-18; 1 Pet. 2:5,9; 1 Tim. 2:5,6; Heb. 4:14-16). No special priesthood is authorized to stand between believers and Christ. Finally, Luther concluded that man can do nothing to merit salvation (Eph. 2:8,9) and, borrowing from Augustine, theorized that he is saved through grace by "faith alone," the fatal flaw of his theology that totally dominated the new Protestant movement.

Reformation, shortly after Luther, broke out in varying degrees in many nations of Europe. Ulrich Zwingli reached similar conclusions in Switzerland, John Calvin in France and Switzerland, Henry VIII in England, John Knox in Scotland, etc. Many theological viewpoints surfaced during the following decades, but three pillars supported the movement: The Bible is the sole authority in matters religious, every believer in Christ is a priest, and salvation is by grace through faith alone.

Origin of Denominationalism. "Faith alone" is the soil in which a harvest of denominational bodies grew. Once theologians accepted the erroneous doctrine of salvation by "faith alone," other matters concerning the New Testament church became secondary and, in many cases, unimportant. If man is saved by "faith alone," then precise church organization is immaterial, exact worship according to truth need not be a prime concern, emphasis on the name of Christ is subject to compromise, baptism as immersion or as essential to salvation is surrendered, and the work of the church is subject to what is judged expedient in each generation.

Issues of these kinds, as one might expect, became optional. Judged to be matters of opinion and human tradition, these qualities varied with each theologian and were reflected in the creeds they wrote and the churches they established. Around those creeds and personal preferences developed scores of Protestant denominations over the next couple of centuries — all differing in work, worship, organization, name, terms of membership, etc.

But all Bible students of the sixteenth century did not see it Luther's way. Men, like Conrad Grebel (c.1498-1526) and Menno Simons (1492-1559), believed in a "restitution" of the first-century church. Apostolic practice, they taught, must be restored and promulgated. "Much more drastically than any of their contemporaries they searched the Scriptures in order to recover the pattern of the early church" (*The Reformation of the Sixteenth Century*, Roland H. Bainton 95).

Restoration: Back to the Bible

More than two and a half centuries later a few Protestants renewed the theme of restitution. Their watchwords were "unity" and "restoration." These men saw the divisions of denominationalism as sin, a clear violation of the biblical plea for unity (see John 17:20,21; 1 Cor. 1:10-13; Eph. 4:1-6). Their solution to the problem was to get "back to the Bible" in both *faith* and *practice*!

Barton W. Stone (1772-1844), a Presbyterian preacher, rejected "Calvinism" and the *Westminster Confession of Faith* and appealed to the Bible as the one source of authority for religious practice. He believed all denominational bodies could be dissolved and all men united as one — provided they cease to accept human creeds as standards of authority and "take the Bible as the only sure guide to heaven" (*The Last Will And Testament of the Springfield Presbytery*, Item 7).

Thomas Campbell (1763-1854), also a Presbyterian preacher, called for a return to the Bible as the creed for God's people. In 1809 Campbell wrote the *Declaration And Address* in which he promoted "simple evangelical Christianity, free from all mixture of human opinions and inventions of men." This demands, he wrote, a recognition "that the Church of Christ upon earth is essentially, intentionally, and constitutionally one"; "that division is a horrid evil fraught with many evils"; "that. . . nothing ought to be inculcated upon Christians as articles of faith; nor required of them as terms of communion, but what is expressly taught and enjoined upon them in the word of God." In short there must be a removal of all the "rubbish of the ages" (theologies and traditions of men) and must be found a "thus saith the Lord" for every practice (*Address*: see Propositions 1,10,12).

Alexander Campbell (1788-1866), Thomas's son, popularized and promulgated the principles enunciated by his father in a publication called *The Christian Baptist*. There, over a period of seven years, he wrote 30 some articles on "A Restoration of the Ancient Order of Things." He came down hard on the "clergy system" and the traditions of men. He staunchly urged men to restore "the ancient order of things" by returning to the practices of the first-century church.

Conclusion

To these men and a many others, the oneness and character of the church Jesus built was as essential as faith in Jesus Christ. Restoring the Lord's church, they believed, would end division, denominationalism, and parties of every kind. It would likewise establish independent local congregations of saints like the ones they read about in Scripture. And, with the Bible as the only authority and guide, all schism among churches would end.

But this happens only if men get "back to the Bible." As Thomas Campbell stated it: "Where the Scriptures speak, we speak; where the Scriptures are silent, we are silent" (*Journey in Faith*, Lester G. McAllister and William E. Tucker 110). The apostle Peter put it just a bit differently: "If any man speak, let him speak as the oracles of God" (1 Pet. 4:11).

The interest of this book, however, is not what Barton W. Stone, Thomas Campbell, or Alexander Campbell thought and wrote. This book seeks to explore the New Testament in search of the true nature and character of the church Jesus built. This demands a return to Bible teaching. It will require a look at the word "church" and "portraits" of the church; it necessitates a look at the "foundation," "beginning," "head," "membership," "name," "structure," "mission," "worship," "purity," and "sufficiency" of the church.

May God bless this exploration and all readers in an effort to get "back to the Bible" and to understand the pristine purity of the New Testament church.

An Outline Study Guide
Introduction:
A. List and discuss modern practices in contrast to biblical teaching. Mass?

Political objectives? Recreation? Gimmicks? Modernism? Don't limit

yourselves to this text. _____

_____

B. Analyze Paul's description of apostasy (1 Tim. 4:1-3; Acts 20:29,30). ___

Apostasy: The Rise of Catholicism:

A. Who was Ignatius and what view did he promote? _____

How far did this departure go? _____

B. How did Ignatius' view violate Scripture (Acts 20:17,28; 1 Pet. 5:1-3)? __

C. What developed alongside the authority of bishops? _____

What does "hierarchy" mean? _____

D. In what practice did priests first assert their authority over worship? _____
What does the "mass" say about the body and blood of Jesus? _____

E. What is a "sacrament"? How many are there? Discuss each briefly. ____

F. List and discuss other doctrinal and moral departures in Catholicism._____

Reformation: The Rise of Denominationalism:

A. When did Martin Luther live and what were the two major doctrinal errors
he first opposed? _____

B. Who provoked Luther's revolt and what was he doing? _____

Define an indulgence. What did it signify in Luther's days? _____

C. How did Luther first show his protest? _____

What were the 95 theses? _____

D. What are the three pillars of Reformation? _____

_____

How many of the pillars are scriptural (2 Tim. 3:16,17; Gal. 1:6-9; 2 John 9; Eph. 2:13-18; 1 Pet. 2:5,9; 1 Tim. 2:5,6; Heb. 4:14-16)? Justify your answer. _____

_____

_____

E. What effect did "faith only" have on the Reformation? _____

_____

_____

D. Were there any defenders of "restoration" in Luther's days? If yes, who were they and what did they emphasize? _____

_____

_____

What was their word for "restoration"? _____

_____

Restoration: Back to the Bible:

A. What were two goals of the restoration movement? _____

_____

B. Why did they think unity was so important (John 17:20,21; 1 Cor. 1:1-13; Eph. 4:1-6)? _____

_____

C. Discuss Barton W. Stone, Thomas Campbell, and Alexander Campbell. What did they write and what was the emphasis of each? _____

_____

_____

Conclusion:

A. What does "restoration" seek to do beyond "faith"? _____

_____

B. Restoration, according to a saying of Thomas Campbell, is possible only if

men: _____

_____

What apostle agreed with this and how did he state it (1 Pet. 4:11)? _____

_____

C. Whose writings will this book emphasize? _____

How would you state the theme of this study? _____

_____

Ekklēsia:
Called out of Darkness

Introduction

Modern English versions of the Bible are extremely readable. Some translations contain few reminders of their Hebrew or Greek origin. The English flows as though the reader were ingesting the original itself. Occasionally, however, the text gives pause for reflection. These are places translators themselves struggle to find the exact English equivalent of a Hebrew or Greek word.

How, for example, should Bible scholars translate the word *denarius*? When the disciples questioned Jesus about paying taxes, the Lord responded: "Show me the tribute money. And they brought unto him a denarius" (Matt. 22:19). *Denarius* is a Latin word incorporated into the Greek text sixteen times. According to a footnote in the American Standard Version (Matt. 18:28), it was a coin worth about $.17 by the standards of 1901. At today's value it may be worth $.67 or $1.33. Who knows. So how should it be translated? "Silver coin" or "penny" (KJV)? "Shilling" or "denarius" (ASV)? "Day's wages" or "denarius" (NIV)? "Dollar" (Goodspeed)? The simple way out is not to translate, but to transliterate the Greek word (*dēnarion*) into English letters — thus "denarius."

Something similar but a bit more complicated happens when translators render the Greek word *ekklēsia* — "church." Many language and biblical scholars are not particularly fond of the term "church" and yet it is retained in most English versions of the New Testament. Since Bible readers meet it in most translations, it is important to understand its origin, its biblical meaning and uses, and its modern connotations and misuses. It is a torturous way to begin a study of the church, but it will give readers a feel for the winding route scholars sometimes follow to provide them God's word in their native tongue.

The word "church," according to the *Oxford English Dictionary*, is probably the Teutonic spelling of the Greek word *kuriakon*, which means "belonging to the Lord" or "of the Lord." *Kuriakon* or *kuriakos* is used twice in the New Testament, once of the "Lord's" supper and once of the "Lord's" day (1 Cor. 11:20; Rev. 1:10) — but never of the "Lord's" people or the church. By the third century or so *kuriakon* meant the "Lord's" house as a place of worship. But when the Teutons transliterated *kuriakon* "church," they used it in place of *ecclēsia*, the Latin spelling of the Greek word — *ekklēsia*.

The word "church," thus, found its way into English versions as a translation of *ekklēsia*, not *kuriakon*. The English word "church," as noted a bit later, is freighted with baggage of human traditions and modern theologies and does not lend itself to an impartial study of the first-century church. An understanding of the church must, therefore, begin with the meaning of *ekklēsia*.

Ekklēsia — Its History

Classical Greek. As early as 425-400 B.C. the word *ekklēsia* described a gathering or assembly of people in Athens or other Greek cities: citizens who had been called together by a herald for discussion of public business. The citizens, an assembly of *ekklētoi* (called ones), were summoned to deliberate over social, political, economic, religious problems that faced the community. This use matches the origin of the word: *ek*, meaning "out of" and *klēsia*, a "calling," hence an assembly of citizens called out or summoned together.

Greek Old Testament. By 275-200 B.C. the Hebrew Old Testament was translated into the Greek Septuagint and the translators faced the difficulty of rendering two Hebrew words of similar meaning: *edah* and *qahal*. The first was primarily translated *sunagōgē*, meaning an assembly brought or gathered together. The second was commonly rendered *ekklēsia*, an assembly called out or summoned together. *Edah* is never translated *ekklēsia*, but *qahal* is sometimes rendered *sunagōgē*. What, then, is the difference between the two Hebrew words? Scholars seem uncertain.

English Old Testament. English translations of the Old Testament also reflect this ambivalence. The King James Version generally renders both *edah* and *qahal* "congregation," but occasionally translates each "assembly." The American Standard translators tried to distinguish the two by translating *edah* "congregation" and *qahal* "assembly." But what difference is intended between these two English words? The New International Version treats the Hebrew words as synonymous, rendering both "community." If no material difference exists between *edah* and *qahal*, *ekklēsia* seems then to denote in the Septuagint the "assembly" or "congregation" or "community" of Israel.

Greek New Testament. In the days of Jesus and the apostles, *ekklēsia*, its uses in the New Testament verify, changed little from its meaning in the Greek Old Testament. It maintains the significance of "assembly" or "congregation," but in application and teaching expresses its inherent idea of the "called out" or gathering of "called ones."

Ekklēsia — Its New Testament Meaning

Ekklēsia appears 114 times in the Greek New Testament: 3 times in the gospels, 23 times in the book of Acts, 68 times in the epistles, and 20 times in Revelation. The King James Version translates it "church" all but three times, where it is rendered "assembly" (Acts 19:32,39,41). The American Standard Version and New International Version follow this pattern with two exceptions — Acts 7:38 and Hebrews 2:12. There *ekklēsia* is translated "congregation."

New Testament Meaning. New Testament writers employ *ekklēsia* 109 times to denote a body of disciples called Christians (Acts 11:26). The term appropriately describes Christians, men and women who have been summoned by God "with a *holy calling*, not according to our works, but according to his own purpose and grace, which was given us in Christ Jesus before times eternal" (2 Tim. 1:9; see 1 Pet. 5:10).

The call of Christians began in preparation when Jesus called his disciples (Luke 6:12-19), ordered them to search for followers in the cities of Judea (Matt. 10:5-15), and issued a general invitation: "Come unto me, all ye that labor and are heavy laden, and I will give you rest. Take my yoke upon you, and learn of me; for I am meek and lowly in heart: and ye shall find rest unto your souls" (Matt. 11:28-30). At the conclusion of his ministry the call went forth in finality and fullness when the Lord sent apostles into all the world to "preach the gospel to the whole creation" and to "make disciples of all nations" (Mark 16:15; Matt. 28:19). By the gospel men are called, for "God chose you from the beginning unto salvation in sanctification of the Spirit and belief of the truth: whereunto *he called you through our gospel*, to the obtaining of the glory of our Lord Jesus Christ" (2 Thess. 2:13,14).

The gospel call is heralded to all men, men who labor beneath the burden of sin under the power of Satan. "All have sinned, and fall short of the glory of God," Paul declared. "There is none righteous, no, not one" (Rom. 3:23; 3:10). To every man, to sinners the Almighty calls: "Come ye out from among them, and be ye separate, saith the Lord, And touch no unclean thing; And I will receive you, And will be to you a Father, and ye shall be to me sons and daughters" (2 Cor. 6:17,18).

Those who answer the call are "an elect race, a royal priesthood, a holy nation, a people for God's own possession, that ye may show forth the excellencies of him who *called you out of darkness into his marvellous light*" (1 Pet. 2:9,10). Saints at Colossae had been "delivered. . . *out of the power of darkness*, and translated. . . into the kingdom of the Son of his love" (Col. 1:13). Saints at Corinth are the "church of God" who *"were called into the fellowship of his Son Jesus Christ our Lord"* (1 Cor. 1:1,2,9).

The word "saint" is a key to understanding God's "holy calling" by the gospel and the meaning of "church," an assembly or congregation of saints. Saint comes from the word "holy" or "sanctified" and is defined negatively and positively. It means both "separateness" from what is common or ordinary and "consecration" to what is special or sacred. Priests of Israel are examples.

These holy men were "set apart" from ordinary citizens of the nation and "consecrated" to the religious services of the tabernacle. They alone were "sanctified" to offer animal sacrifices, burn incense, light the tabernacle candles, display the showbread, etc.

So the *ekklēsia* is a body of special people: citizens who are "set apart" from the common life of the world and enrolled in the heavenly city (see Phil. 3:20; Heb. 12:22,23). As citizens of heaven they are "consecrated" to the one who sits at God's right hand and issued orders from above (see Col. 3:1,2). Only those who answer the call of the gospel to separate from the carnal life of sin and to walk worthily of the gospel constitute the faithful *ekklēsia*. These are they who are "called out of darkness" and "into the fellowship of his Son Jesus Christ"; they are the "congregation" or "assembly" or "community" of God in Christ (see again 1 Pet. 2:9,10; 1 Cor. 1:9).

Ekklēsia — Its New Testament Uses

Civic Assembly. Ekklēsia occurs once in Scripture with reference to a civic assembly, common among the Greeks. Luke wrote of the "regular assembly" at Ephesus that often convened to discuss the business of the community (Acts 19:39). Thayer calls it "an assembly of the people convened at the public place of council for the purpose of deliberating."

Tumultuous Mob. Circumstances arose in Ephesus that the community viewed as a threat to their religious and economic stability. The apostle Paul had preached against idolatry and masses of citizens turned to the living God in rejection of Diana, the goddess of the Ephesians. A crowd of civic-minded Ephesians assembled into an angry mob — an *ekklēsia*. So Luke described it (Acts 19:31,41). Thayer defines it as "any gathering or throng of men assembled by chance or tumultuously."

Jewish Congregation. "In the Septuagint often equivalent to *qahal*. . .an assembly of Israelites, Judg. 21:8; 1 Chron. 29:1, etc; especially when gathered for sacred purposes, Deut. 31:30. . .Josh. 8:35. . .etc.; *in the New Testament thus in Acts 7:38; Heb. 2:12*" (Thayer). Stephen's speech to Jews at Jerusalem includes a reference to Moses as leader of Israel — "who was in the *congregation* [*ekklēsia*] in the wilderness with the angel who spoke to him on Mt. Sinai" (Acts 7:38). The *ekklēsia* here is the nation of Israel whom God selected and called from the midst of other nations to be a chosen people consecrated to him and his will (Exod. 19:3-6; Deut. 7:6). Another reference to the nation is found in Psalms 22:22 and is quoted in Hebrews 2:12, where the writer spoke of singing God's praises in the *congregation* — *ekklēsia*.

Ekklēsia in the remainder of the New Testament denotes the spiritual body of Christians who are committed to separation from the darkness of sin and to service under the will of Christ. But even here four different applications are found.

Universal Church. The universal church, in Thayer's words, is "the whole body of Christians scattered throughout the earth, collectively, all who worship and honor God and Christ in whatever place they be." When Jesus promised "upon this rock I will build my church," he referred to the church generally — the composite of all who respond to the gospel call. The writer of Hebrews spoke of the universal church as "the general assembly and church of the firstborn." He wrote not of the totality of congregations throughout the world, as some erroneously suppose, but to the sum of individual Christians worldwide: to all "who are enrolled in heaven" (see Heb. 12:23). Every Christian's name is written in heaven and they all together constitute the universal church.

Local Church. "Those," Thayer says of local churches, "who anywhere, in city or village, constitute such a company and are united in one body." The local church is a specific group of Christians who are in the same geographical area and have purposed to band and assemble together as a body to fulfill specific goals and needs. Paul wrote to the "church of God which is at Corinth" and "the church of the Thessalonians" (1 Cor. 1:2; 1 Thess. 1:1), using the word to identify a limited, local group of saints.

Unassembled. Ekklēsia does not of itself specify a local church that is physically assembled. Christians constitute the church when they are assembled or at their homes. Saul of Tarsus made "havoc of the church, entering every house, and dragging off men and women, committing them to prison" (Acts 8:3). Members of the *ekklēsia* at Jerusalem, Corinth or Thessalonica are the spiritual body of Christ in those localities, whether assembled or in their homes.

Assembled. Ekklēsia also refers to an actual assembly of the disciples. Five times in one passage Paul wrote of the brethren at Corinth coming together to observe the Lord's supper (1 Cor. 11:17,18,20,33,34). One of those verses describes a coming "together in the *ekklēsia*" (1 Cor. 11:18). Three chapters later the apostle used the word *ekklēsia* several times to denote the assembled body of brethren for worship and edification (1 Cor. 14:19,33,34,35).

Regional. Finally, *ekklēsia* denotes saints who reside in a specific region of the world. It is employed in the distributive sense of all Christians of a region, if as some manuscripts have it, Luke used the singular number — "the church throughout all Judea and Galilee and Samaria" (Acts 9:31). If, on the other hand, as most manuscripts read, the plural number is correct, Luke refers to all local congregations in those regions (for plural use see also Acts 15:41; Rom. 16:4; 1 Cor. 16:1,19; Gal. 1:2,22; 1 Thess. 2:14; Rev. 1:4,11,20).

What is important is that the word *ekklēsia*, contrary to many modern abuses, always described people — a body of people, locally or universally, who had answered the call of the gospel to leave the bondage and practice of sin and enter fellowship with God and Christ to walk in light. They, as a result, are called the "church of God," "churches of Christ," "churches of God in Christ," or, more simply, "the church."

Conclusion — Contemporary Misuses of "Church"

Contemporary misuses of the word "church" must be noted before moving further into this study. They are summed up neatly in *Webster's Collegiate Dictionary*. The only biblically correct definition found in Webster is: "The collective body of Christians." All others are abuses of the term.

The word "church" is never used in Scripture, as Webster defines it, to refer to: (1) "a building for public worship"; (2) "church services; divine worship"; (3) "the organization of Christianity, as in a nation; esp., ecclesiastical power or government"; (4) "the clerical profession"; (5) "a body of Christian believers having the same creed, rites, etc; a denomination; as, the Presbyterian Church"; (6) "any body of worshipers; a religious society."

When readers eliminate these modern concepts of the church from their thinking, they will be prepared with open minds to grasp the nature and character of the first-century church. That is the goal of the remaining lessons of this book.

An Outline Study Guide

Introduction:

A. Discuss the translation problem of *denarius*. How do translators render it?

_____

B. Discuss the origin of the word "church." _____

What does *kuriakon* mean and how is it used in Scripture? _____

_____

What Greek word does "church" translate in the New Testament? _____

Ekklēsia — Its History:

A. How was *ekklēsia* used by ancient Greeks? _____

B. What is the Septuagint?_____

What Hebrew words did *ekklēsia* translate in the Septuagint? _____

_____ What difference is there between these two

words? _____

_____

C. What did *ekklēsia* mean in the Old Testament? _____

What English words are equivalent to *ekklēsia* in the Old Testament? _____

D. Break down the word *ekklēsia* and discuss its original meaning._____

_____

Ekklēsia — Its New Testament Meaning:

A. How many times does *ekklēsia* occur in the New Testament? _____

The Gospels? _____ Acts? _____ Epistles? _____ Revelation?_____

B. How many times does it refer to the body of Christ? _____

C. How does its root meaning relate to Christians (2 Tim. 1:9; 1 Pet. 5:10)?

_____

By what are Christians called (2 Thess. 2:13,14)? _____

Out of what are they called? _____ Into what are they called? __

_____

D. Relate the word "saint" to meaning of *ekklēsia*. What does "saint" mean — negatively and positively? _____

_____

E. Describe the saint's citizenship and relate it to *ekklēsia*. _____

_____

Ekklēsia — Its New Testament Use:

A. Acts 19:39: How is *ekklēsia* used here? _____

B. Acts 19:32,41: Give the background, its significance, and use here. _____

_____

C. Acts 7:38; Hebrews 2:12: How is it translated here in KJV? _____

NKJV _____ NASB _____ NIV _____

To what does it refer in each text? _____

D. Matthew 16:18; Ephesians 1:22,23: How would you describe its use here?

_____

_____

E. 1 Corinthians 1:2; 1 Thessalonians 1:1: Contrast its use here with Matthew 16:18. _____

F. What difference do you see in it uses in Acts 8:3 and 1 Corinthians 11:18; 14:19,33,34,35? _____

G. Acts 9:31: What does *ekklēsia* mean here — if singular? _____

    If plural? _____

Conclusion — Contemporary Misuses:
A. What correct definition does Webster give? _____

B. List and discuss the scripturalness or unscripturalness of the word "church" as a: Building; Worship Services; Church/State; Clergy; Denomination; Religious Society. _____

_____

_____

C. Why can one not rely on Webster to define accurately the biblical meaning of the word "church"? _____

_____

Relationships:
Portraits of the Church

Introduction

Life, when lived responsibly and fully, is neither simple nor easy. It is a complex of many relationships that demand time, skill, duty, and many other qualities. At one moment man is an employee seeking to please his employer and at another a citizen striving to fulfill civic duties. Beyond this and more importantly, Mr. Employee or Mr. Citizen must relate sacrificially as a husband to his wife, lovingly as a father to his children, and honorably as a son to his aged parents. He is one person with many roles.

Similarly, Christians are viewed as *disciples* who must learn of Christ and follow in his footsteps; *saints* who are set apart from evil and consecrated to God's sacred word; *priests* who are charged with offering themselves and their bodies as spiritual sacrifices to God through Christ Jesus; *bondservants* who must subdue their will in interest of the will of their Master in heaven; *believers* who walk by faith and trust in Christ for unseen blessings of hope. Each word contains its own portrait of God's children and, combined, depicts the variety of relationships and roles they accept as men and women in Christ. So it is with the church as a company of Christians.

The church is a congregation or assembly of people who have answered the call of the gospel to come out of the world and live separately from sin (2 Cor. 6:17; 1 Pet. 2:9,10). They have consecrated themselves to God as a peculiar people zealous of good works (Tit. 2:11-14). Their names have been written in heaven and their lives reflect the qualities of the God who called them by the gospel (see Heb. 12:22,23; Col. 3:1,2). This the very word "church" conveys.

As the church the lives of the members move in many directions and work out many relationships. The Lord pictured those relationships in a variety of figures. The church is viewed as a "body," a "kingdom," a "temple," a "household"; each of these images mirrors fundamental obligations and duties. It is both enlightening and significant that the church understands each of these portraits of itself.

The Body

And he put all things in subjection under his feet, and gave him to be head

over all things to the *church, which is his body*, the fulness of him that filleth
all in all (Eph. 1:22,23)

Three important passages of Scripture discuss the church as a body: Romans
12:4-8; 1 Corinthians 12:12-31; Ephesians 4:11-16. The reference is to the
human body, consisting of its head and diverse members. The emphasis is on
Christ as the head, the church as the body, and each Christian as a member.

Head. When Jesus ascended into the heavens to the right hand of God, the
Father "gave him to be head over all things to the church, which is his body."
This truth reveals three ideas: (1) The church is Christ's body; (2) Christ controls
the church; (3) The church is subject to Christ. Man's body follows the direction
of its head and the church follows Christ. The church is no monstrosity with two
heads — one on earth and one in heaven. The church submits only to Christ.

Paul stated this specifically when he compared the relationship of husband
and wife to Christ and the church. "For the husband is head of the wife as
Christ also is the head of the church. . . But as the church is subject to Christ,
so let the wives also be to their husbands in everything" (Eph. 5:23,24). The
church is not a "loose cannon"; it is tightly controlled and directed; its activities
are patterned after the divine plan of its Head. The church is not what members
want it to be, but what Christ designed it to be. It submits itself to Christ "in
everything."

Members. The church, a body, consists of many members. Man's body has
eyes, ears, nose, feet, hands, etc. — all of which are vital to its many functions.
"For the body is not one member, but many" (1 Cor. 12:14). And that body
functions when each member recognizes and performs its own role and respects
the role of others. "All members have not the same office [work]" (Rom. 12:4).

No member may be jealous of another. The foot does not reject its role in
the body because it is not the hand. So with the ears toward the eyes and so on.
How could the body work if the entire unit were an eye or an ear? If it were
wholly an eye, where would be the smelling, or, if a nose, where would be the
hearing or seeing? The body works precisely because it is many members and
each fulfills its role (see 1 Cor. 12:15-20).

No member may reject another. The eye may not say to the hand, "I have
no need of thee." Nor may the head say to the feet, "I have no need of you."
Even the members of the body that seem more feeble or less honorable must be
respected. There must be no schism in the body and each member cares for
every other member. When one member suffers, all suffer; when one is
honored, all rejoice (see 1 Cor. 12:21-26).

The body functions properly because of its diversity. A variety of talents
enables the church to meet all essential needs. If, as men were endowed in the
first century, a man is an apostle or prophet, let him do that work. And let no
one be jealous of his accomplishments and God forbid that he should denigrate

the work of others less gifted. Those who can teach — let them teach; so also those who can preach, pastor, exhort, give, sympathize, serve, etc. (see Rom. 12:6-8).

The goal of the body and its variety of gifts is "the perfecting of the saints" — the equipping of them for service. When equipped they can perform the "work of ministering" and the "building up of the body of Christ." This strengthens each member and increases the spirituality of all till they arrive unto a "measure of the stature of the fulness of Christ." No longer tossed to and fro by every wind of doctrine through the deceitfulness of men, they are built up by truth in love through that which every joint and part of the body supplies (see Eph. 4:11-16).

The church is a "body," a unit subject to Christ. Members submit to his will, are fitly framed and knit together with other members, and by their gifts strengthen and fortify the whole. Members one of another, they love one another (Rom. 13:8), edify one another (Rom. 14:19), comfort one another (1 Thess. 4:18), admonish one another (Rom. 15:14), serve one another (Gal. 5:13), bear one another's burdens (Gal. 6:2), forgive one another (Eph. 4:32), etc.

The Kingdom

> Worthy are thou to take the book, and to open the seals thereof: for thou wast slain, and didst purchase unto God with thy blood men of every tribe, and tongue, and people, and nation, and *madest them to be unto our God a kingdom* and priests; and they reign on the earth (Rev. 5:9,10).

Serious Bible students know that "kingdom" and "church" are not always synonymous ideas and do not in all cases denote exactly the same thing. Those same students, however, should recognize that "kingdom" does in some instances describe the people known as the "church." The verses above are but one example. Here "kingdom" describes people purchased by the blood of Christ, the redeemed and forgiven ones in Christ. Revelation 5:9,10 parallels Acts 20:28, where Paul speaks of the "church of the Lord which he purchased with his own blood." "Kingdom" and "church," in this respect, are employed in the universal sense of all saved ones in Christ. But what does the "kingdom" idea reveal about the people of God?

King. Kingdoms are ruled by "kings," and citizens are subjects to royal authority. The "kingdom of God," the "kingdom of his dear Son" or the "kingdom of Christ and God" is the domain of Christians who honor the sovereignty of Jesus and submit to the will of "the King of kings and Lord of lords" (see Acts 8:12; Col. 1:13; Eph. 5:5; Rev. 1:5; 17:14). God raised Jesus to his right hand, exalted him above all rule and power and authority, and crowned him "Lord and Christ." Jesus possesses "all authority" in heaven and on earth and his will reigns supreme (Acts 2:33-36; Eph. 1:20-23; Matt. 28:18).

Citizens. While in a broad sense all is subject to Christ, even "the uttermost parts of the earth," the redeemed subjects of the spiritual kingdom are they who have come "to the city of the living God, the heavenly Jerusalem. . . to the general assembly and church of the firstborn who are enrolled in heaven" (Heb. 12:22,23). There they have received a "kingdom that cannot be shaken" (Heb. 12:28). There citizenship is heavenly and their minds are set on things above where Christ is seated at God's right hand (Phil. 3:20; Col. 3:2). They are a kingdom "not of this world" (John 18:36). Citizens of Christ's kingdom are born anew by water and the Spirit; begotten again by incorruptible seed, the word of God; new creatures who by faith have been baptized into Christ and have arisen to walk a new life (see John 3:3-5; 1 Pet. 1:22,23; 2 Cor. 5:17; Gal. 3:26,27; Rom. 6:3,4).

Realm. Jesus detailed this re-creative process in his most basic parable. The kingdom of heaven is like a sower who went forth to sow seed in a field. Some seed fell on good ground. The seed is "the word of God" or "the word of the kingdom" and the rich soil is "an honest and good heart," which produces fruit of 100, 60, and 30 fold. The realm of the King's rule, the parable vividly illustrates, is men's hearts, where the Lord's truths, ideas, and will are rooted and in control. The rule comes not with observation; not with marching armies, clanging swords, or pounding horses' hooves — but with the silent, secret working of eternal principles in receptive hearts of spiritual men (see Luke 8:4-15; Matt. 13:3-9, 18-23; Luke 17:20,21). The seed sprouts, blossoms, and bears the fruit of righteousness, purity, holiness, and love (see Phil. 1:9-11; Gal. 5:22,23).

Saints, holy men of God, were added to the "*church* of God which is at Corinth" and saints at Colossae were delivered "out of the power of darkness and translated...into the *kingdom* of the Son of his love" (see 1 Cor. 1:1,2; Col. 1:1,13). Men who switch allegiance, who reject the authority of darkness and sin and submit to the royal law of love, who out of love keep the commands of God's heavenly king — these are the royal priesthood, the holy nation, the peculiar possession of God. The church sees itself as royal subjects to heaven's will — citizens who each day pray, "thy will be done" (see 1 Pet. 2:9,10; Matt. 22:37-39; Jas. 2:8-11; John. 14:15; Matt. 6:10).

Temple

Know ye not that ye are a temple of God, and that the Spirit of God dwelleth in you? If any man destroyeth the temple of God, him shall God destroy; for the temple of God is holy, and such are ye (1 Cor. 3:16,17).

The "temple" figure draws from the Old Testament, where the tabernacle and Solomon's temple foreshadowed a spiritual dwelling place of God through the Spirit. The tabernacle and the temple were the places of divine service: where the holy priesthood entered to present offerings to God and the glory of God appeared once a year on the day of atonement. Both were sacred dwelling places for God (see Exod. 40; 2 Chron. 7).

Peter alluded to this in his description of Christians as a "holy priesthood" designed "to offer up spiritual sacrifices, acceptable to God through Jesus Christ." Christ is "a living stone" who was rejected of men but with God elect and precious and was made the "chief corner stone" or "head of the corner." Christians are "living stones" who are "built up to be a spiritual house." They are a "priesthood" to offer divine services and a "spiritual house" in whom God dwells (1 Pet. 2:3-11).

The apostle Paul wrote to the Ephesians about the "foundation of the apostles and prophets, Christ Jesus himself being the chief corner stone." Christians are built on this foundation — "fitly framed together" and "groweth into a holy temple in the Lord." They "are builded together for a habitation of God in the Spirit" (Eph. 2:20-22; see also 1 Cor. 3:16).

The church as God's temple means three things: (1) Christians are stones built on Christ, the foundation of truth revealed by holy apostles and prophets; (2) A spiritual house that is sacred and holy — separated from all defilement and dedicated to God; (3) A dwelling place of God, signifying fellowship with and reconciliation to God by the gospel. Outside the church men have no portion with God and the blessings of Christ.

Household of God

These things write I unto thee, hoping to come unto thee shortly; but if I tarry long, that thou mayest know how men ought to behave themselves in the *house of God, which is the church of the living God*, the pillar and ground of the truth (1 Tim. 3:14,15).

"House" may mean a dwelling place or a family relationship. Jesus spoke figuratively of a dwelling place in the conclusion of the sermon on the mount and Peter, as just observed, wrote about a "spiritual house" as a dwelling built upon Christ (Matt. 7:24-27; 1 Pet. 2:4,5). Numbers of other references, however, describe a family relationship (see Acts 16:31; 18:8; 1 Tim. 3:4,5).

God's house is his family and Christ is "a son over his house; whose house are we, if we hold fast our boldness and the glorying of our hope firm unto the end" (Heb. 3:6). "So then ye are no more strangers and sojourners, but ye are fellow-citizens with the saints, and *of the household of God*" (Eph. 2:19).

Father. God's household, the church, enjoys fellowship with God their Father and, as a result of this relationship, may address him in prayer: "Our Father who art in heaven" (Matt. 6:9). In answer he provides their needs (Matt. 6:33; Heb. 4:14-16), gives them comfort (2 Cor. 1:3), disciplines them (Heb. 12:4-11), and assures them of an inheritance (Rom. 8:17).

Children. The beauty of a child's status in God's family is that he is there by adoption. All men were slaves, bondservants of sin, until by Christ they were rescued from bondage. Trusting the Lord, they became sons of God by faith when baptized into Christ and into his death (Gal. 3:26,27; Rom. 6:3,4). They received the spirit of adoption and God sent the Spirit of his Son into their hearts crying, "Abba, Father" (see Rom. 8:15; Gal. 4:6). Children of God are "heirs of God, and joint-heirs with Christ" (Rom. 8:17).

Brothers/Sisters. Out of this relationship with God comes responsibility to other children of God as brothers and sisters. Christians are, indeed, their brother's keeper. They are to convert him from the error of his ways (Jas. 5:19,20), restore him when overtaken with a trespass (Gal. 6:1), bear with him his unbearable burdens (Gal. 6:2), forgive him (Eph. 4:32), and reprove, rebuke, and exhort him (2 Tim. 4:2,3). In short, love him and be kindly affectionate toward him (Rom. 13:8; 12:10). Feed him when he is hungry, clothe him when he is naked, and give him a drink when he is thirsty (see Matt. 25:31-40).

The church, God's family, will reverence and respect God as their heavenly Father, seek his help and accept his discipline, and love and care for fellow brothers and sisters.

Conclusion

Pictures are indeed worth a thousand words. Political cartoonists in pungent and poignant drawings speak volumes, and have been known to influence an entire nation and change the course of history. Pictures of Somolia needed no words to win the hearts of Americans and move the wealthiest and mightiest nation of earth to intervene for the sake of starving humanity.

Jesus knew the power of visual images and provoked the hearts of thousands by the simplicity and imagery of parables. So his apostles spoke to the church with the vivid portraits of — a body, a kingdom, a temple, a family. Here a multiplicity of relationships, responsibilities, and roles are graphically drawn. Look long and hard and then relook at those portraits. See in them the character of God's people as a community of believers.

An Outline Study Guide

Introduction:

A. Enumerate and discuss the variety of relationships in life. _____

_____

B. Summarize the relationships of Christians implied in:

Disciple _____

Saint _____

    Priest _____

    Bondservant _____

C. What relationship is in the word "church"? _____

The Body:

A. What three ideas are suggested by Christ as "head of the church"? _____

    _____

B. What relationship does Paul use to illustrate headship (Eph. 5:23,24)? ____

    _____

    How extensive is the church's subjection to Christ? _____

C. Summarize and detail Paul's illustration of jealousy (1 Cor. 12:15-20). ___

    _____

D. What does Paul say about members rejecting one another (1 Cor. 12:21-26)?

    _____

E. Discuss the diversity of the body and its functions (Rom. 12:6-8). _____

    _____

F. What are the goals of the body's various parts working together (Eph. 4:11-
    16)? _____

    _____

The Kingdom:

A. Show the sense in which "kingdom" and "church" are identical (Rom.
    5:9,10; Acts 20:28). _____

    _____

B. Discuss the King's authority and its breadth. _____

    _____

C. Who are the citizens of the kingdom? Explain the new birth (Heb.
    12:22,23,28; John 3:5; 1 Pet. 1:22,23; 2 Cor. 5:17; Rom. 6:3,4). _____

    _____

D. What is the realm of the King's rule (Luke 8:11-15; Matt. 13:18-23; Luke

17:20,21)? Explain the nature of the kingdom. _____

_____

E. How do 1 Corinthians 1:1,2 and Colossians 1:1,13 show that the "kingdom"
    and "church" denote the same people? _____

_____

The Temple:

A. Where is the portrait of "temple" illustrated and what does it teach? _____

_____

B. What are Christians in the temple and on what are they built (1 Pet. 2:3-11)?

_____

C. Discuss the priesthood. Who are they and what do they offer (1 Pet. 2:5;
    Rom. 12:1)? _____

_____

D. Summarize and discuss the three major ideas emphasized in this portrait. _

_____

The Household:

A. What two ways is the word "house" used in Scripture (1 Pet. 2:4,5; 1 Tim.
    3:4,5)? _____

_____

B. As the family of God what three relationships exist? _____

_____

C. What does God as Father provide (Matt. 6:33; Eph. 1:3; 2 Cor. 1:3; Heb.
    12:4-11; Rom. 8:17)? _____

D. How do men and women become children of God and what is their ultimate
    reward (Gal. 3:26,27; Rom. 8:15-17)? _____

_____

E. Discuss mutual responsibilities of brothers and sisters. _____

_____

Conclusion:

A. Discuss pictures and illustrate their power. _____

_____

B. Describe how Jesus used imagery. _____

_____

C. What in summary do biblical portraits of the church say to brethren? _____

_____

Foundation:
Upon This Rock

Introduction

The secularization of America, deterioration of family life, and erosion of morality threaten to undermine the stability of this once proud country. Lack of faith in God and failure to submit to basic principles of righteousness can only weaken a society that must in time collapse under the weight of increased lawlessness, violence, and neighborly disregard. A nation that feeds on self indulgence, increased dependence on fleshly lust, and insatiable appetite for mammon is built on a shaky foundation of sand.

National life that defies the wisdom of God is doomed to crumble into ruin. The world of Noah found this out when universal violence and wickedness prevailed (Gen. 6:5-7); the cities of Sodom and Gomorrah when perversion and promiscuous lust knew no limits (Gen. 19); the Amorites when iniquity was full and abundant (Gen. 15:16); Israel and Judah when idolatry, social injustice, heartless worship, and immorality inundated the land (2 Kings 17-25). "Righteousness exalteth a nation; But sin is a reproach to any people" (Prov. 14:34).

Religious men, especially those called the religious right, acknowledge this principle when speaking of this crumbling nation. They speak vehemently against abortion, homosexuality, drugs, adultery, political bribery, feminism, elimination of prayer in the schools, and many other moral issues. But the same men take liberties with the authority and doctrine of Christ when the character of the first-century church is at issue. The church, as nations, cannot withstand God's judgment unless it is built on the sure foundation of God's wisdom.

The church is God's spiritual house and any house is only as strong as its foundation. "Ye are," Paul said to the Corinthians, "God's building" — "the temple of God" in which his Spirit dwells. He himself as a wise masterbuilder had laid the foundation there and others had built thereon. And just what is the foundation the apostle laid? And how are durable materials of gold, silver, and costly stones built into God's house (see 1 Cor. 3:10-16)? Let the Lord himself answer.

Rock or Sand

On two occasions Jesus spoke of a foundation of rock. First, the Sermon on the Mount. Here Jesus taught many startling ideas, especially in rebuke of the heartless formalism of Pharisaic life. But what really astonished the audience was his teaching "as one having authority" (Matt. 7:29). The scribes did not teach that way. They enforced law or tradition because Moses taught it, or Isaiah said it, or the fathers handed it down. But again and again Jesus said, "Ye have heard that it was said. . . but *I say* unto you" (Matt. 5:21,22,27,28). "I say" were the words that amazed them. A matter is right or wrong because "I say" so. He needed no backing from rabbis or scribes or chief priests. He himself, because of who he is, is the authority. God confirmed this at his transfiguration: "This is my beloved Son, in whom I am well-pleased; *Hear ye him!"* (Matt. 17:5)

The Son of God and Master Teacher concluded his point on authority with a story about two men — one wise and one foolish. The wise man built his house upon the rock. The foolish man built his house upon the sand. The difference? The wise man is he "that heareth these words of mine, and doeth them" (Matt. 7:24). When storms and trials and afflictions crash against him, his life in the Lord will stand. The foolish man is he "that heareth these words of mine, and doeth them not" (Matt. 7:26). The winds and torrents and turbulence will descend on him and his life will disintegrate to nothing. Respect for the authority of Christ and submission to his will — this simple truth — is the sure foundation for life here and hereafter.

Upon This Rock

Much later in his public ministry Jesus spoke of the sure foundation in a question and answer session with the disciples. He examined and challenged them about his identity. "Who do men say that the Son of man is?" he asked. The answers among the general population included John the Baptist, Elijah, Jeremiah, or one of the prophets. Jesus then asked the disciples directly: "But who say ye that I am?" Simon Peter was the first to reply: "Thou art the Christ, the Son of the living God." To this Jesus responded: "And I also say unto thee, that thou art Peter, and *upon this rock* I will build my church" (Matt. 16:13-18).

One would normally speak of *convening* a church or assembly, but the Lord's first reference to the church evokes the image of constructing a building. "Upon this rock" suggests a foundation and "build" implies erection of a structure. And just what is "this rock," this foundation on which Jesus promised to build his church? Catholic scholars have for centuries affirmed that the rock is Peter, whom the Lord himself confessed. The argument contends that the name Peter (*Petros*) means "rock" and that Jesus is saying, "Thou art a rock" and upon "this rock (*petra*)" the church will be built.

Grammatically, it is possible to identify Peter by name (*Petros*), which does mean rock or stone, and then metaphorically depict him as a ledge of rock (*petra*) on which the church would be built. But logically, historically, contextually, and biblically the position will not stand.

Logically, if the church is built on Peter, it is founded on a man with all the weaknesses of the flesh. Peter specifically showed lack of faith when walking on water, cowardice when denying the Lord three times, and instability when facing the racial and political maneuvering of Jews against Gentiles. Can one who, in the words of Paul, walked "not uprightly according to the truth" be a sure foundation for the church (Matt. 14:22-33; 26:69-75; Gal. 2:11-14)?

Historically, the argument that Peter is the rock comes much too late. New Testament documents do not remotely allude to Peter as the rock on which the church was built. More than a century later bishops had been exalted above elders, apostate bodies had formed, and episcopal authority was deemed necessary to combat error and control the churches. Theologians began using Matthew 16:18 to assert the authority of Peter and all bishops. "It was in fact, Tertullian [A. D. 198]. . . who took in hand the speculative interpretation of the famous New Testament texts — *Tu es Petrus* [Thou art Peter, LAS], and the like — which established the unique prerogatives of Peter as the first of apostles" (*The Medieval Papacy*, Geoffrey Barraclough 15). The argument made today by Catholic theologians for Peter's primacy was not, according to Barraclough, perfected until Leo I, bishop of Rome from A. D. 440-461 (*Ibid.* 26,27).

Contextually, the subject of Matthew 16:18 is not Peter but the identity of Jesus. Who do people in general say Jesus is? Who do the disciples believe he is? That is the question. The answer, revealed not by flesh and blood but by God the Father, is given in Peter's confession: "Thou art the Christ, the Son of the living God" (Matt. 16:16). The Christ, God's Son — who and what he is — is the "rock" upon which the church is built. He, both prophecy and New Testament teaching confirm, is the sure foundation, tried stone, precious stone, and chief cornerstone. Anyone or anything else is sand.

A Sure Foundation

Biblically. A study of the sure foundation takes Bible students back to a prophecy by Isaiah. "Behold, I lay in Zion for a foundation a stone, a tried stone, a precious corner stone of sure foundation" (Isa. 28:16). Did the prophet promise a foundation for building a temple in physical Jerusalem, or did he envision another foundation? New Testament application provides an indisputable answer.

Stone/Jesus. The apostle Paul combined Isaiah 28:16 with Isaiah 8:14 to describe Jesus as "a stone of stumbling and rock of offence" to the Jews who refused to believe in him (Rom. 9:33; 10:11). Jesus is the stone in Zion over which Jews stumbled in unbelief. Peter made the same application, portraying

Jesus as "a living stone, rejected indeed of men, but with God elect, precious." Those who believe on him are "living stones" who are built upon him as a spiritual house; to them he is a precious stone. But to those who disbelieve, are disobedient, and stumble at the word, he is "the stone which the builders rejected," "a stone of stumbling," "a rock of offence" (1 Pet. 2:4-8).

Zion/Church. Zion is not the literal hill in Jerusalem, but the holy hill in heavenly places where God dwells and his king rules. There God set the Messiah at his own right hand, who now rules with the rod of his strength as "King of kings and Lord of lords" (see Psa. 2:6,7; 110:1,2; Acts 2:33-36; Rev. 17:14). When men and women come to God, to the heavenly Jerusalem, to the church of the firstborn, to Jesus the mediator of a new covenant — they come to mount Zion where the rejected stone became the head of the corner (Heb. 12:22-24; Acts 4:11,12; Eph. 2:20-22).

Tried Stone. The sure foundation laid in Zion was a "tried stone" — one that, as metal, had been tested and proved to be of enduring quality; a stone that showed no weakness; one that would not crush or crumble beneath the weighty trials of life. Jesus, the tried stone, was "a man approved of God unto you by mighty works, and wonders, and signs" (Acts 2:22). But how was Jesus tested and why did God approve of him?

His character was tested. Made like unto man, he was "in all points tempted like as we are, yet without sin" (Heb. 4:15). When the Spirit led the Son of God into the wilderness, Satan was not far behind. There the old deceiver and roaring lion approached Jesus, tested him, and found no weakness of the flesh. Jesus refused to be drawn away by the lust of the flesh, the lust of the eyes, or the pride of life (see Jas. 1:13-15; 1 John 2:15-17). He withstood the onslaught of the devil on every front and challenged the generation of Jews among whom he lived: "Which of you convicteth me of sin?" (John 8:46) Not one made a valid charge against him. One of his own apostles declared that he "did no sin, neither was guile found in his mouth" (1 Pet. 2:22). By his example God's only Son set before a world of weakness and sin a "sure" foundation for life.

His will was tested. "Lo, I am come. . . to do thy will, O God. . . By which will we have been sanctified through the offering of the body of Jesus Christ once for all" (Heb. 10:7,10). "My meat is to do the will of him that sent me, and to accomplish his work" (John 4:34). Jesus' will to obey the Father was tried severely in the garden of Gethsemane, where he faced the ultimate challenge. He must die for the sins of the world; not just die, yea the death of the cross (see Phil. 2:8). He prayed three times for the cup of death to pass — if possible. He agonized over his upcoming death; he sweated as it were great drops of blood. But each prayer expressed the commitment — "thy will be done" (Matt. 26:36-44). When God said "no" the third time, Jesus arose, faced his captors, and surrendered to arrest, trial, and crucifixion.

His claim was tested. Was Jesus more than a man? Was he really the Son of God? Surely, miracles confirmed that claim (John 20:30,31). Was he really the bread and water of life that sustain men forever? Only a bout with death and a victory could establish that. He alluded to victory over death when he assured the disciples that "the gates of Hades shall not prevail against" the building of the church (Matt. 16:18). "Thou wilt not leave my soul in Hades, neither wilt thou give thy Holy One to see corruption" were the words of the Psalmist as quoted by Peter at Pentecost. The apostle applied these words to the resurrection of Jesus: that his spirit did not remain in the unseen realm of Hades and his body did not corrupt in the grave (see Psa. 16:10 and Acts 2:25-32).

He was the "rejected stone" that became the "head of the corner" (Psa. 118:22; see Matt. 21:33-46; Acts 4:11; 1 Pet. 2:4). Rejected of men and condemned as a blasphemer, he was nailed to the cross as a common criminal. But death and Hades could not prevail and the sealing of the tomb was a futile act of unbelief. On the third day, as he had so often announced, the stone was rolled away, the tomb was empty, and he began appearing to more than 500 brethren. He had come forth to build his church and become the head of the corner — "the foundation of the apostles and prophets, Christ Jesus being the chief cornerstone" (Eph. 2:20).

Jesus passed the greatest test of all and "was declared to be the Son of God with power, according to the spirit of holiness, by the resurrection from the dead" (Rom. 1:4). The apostle John, in the visions of Revelation, saw one like unto a son of man amidst the seven churches. Arrayed in a priestly or royal garment, the son spoke comforting words to those maligned and persecuted churches: "Fear not; I am the first and the last, and the Living one; and I was dead, and behold, I am alive for evermore, and I have the keys of death and of Hades" (Rev. 1:17,18). As the tried stone, rejected stone, precious stone, chief cornerstone, Jesus is the sure foundation who has the keys and power of life and death.

No Other Foundation

Many in the church at Corinth had soon removed themselves from the sure foundation. Enamored by human wisdom and divided in their loyalty to Christ, some said: "I am of Paul; and I of Apollos; and I of Cephas [Peter]; and I of Christ" (1 Cor. 1:12). And who are these men? "Ministers through whom ye believed, and each as the Lord gave to him" (1 Cor. 3:5). Paul then charged them with being "carnal" and walking "after the manner of men" (1 Cor. 3:3). After a severe rebuke the apostle reminded them of the foundation laid in Corinth:

> According to the grace of God which was given unto me, as a wise
> masterbuilder I laid a foundation; and another buildeth thereon. But let each
> man take heed how he buildeth thereon. *For other foundation can no man lay*

than that which is laid, which is Jesus Christ (1 Cor. 3:10,11).

The sure and only foundation is Jesus Christ. It is not Paul, Peter, Apollos, or any other man. That foundation Paul himself laid when he came to Corinth. Luke recorded that visit in Acts. "But when Silas and Timothy came down from Macedonia, Paul was constrained by the word testifying to the Jews that *Jesus was the Christ*" (Acts 18:5). The message Paul preached is the confession Peter made: Jesus is the Christ. "Upon this rock," Jesus said of Peter's confession, "I will build my church." Paul said of the Christ, "Other foundation can no man lay."

Conclusion

Living stones are built on the sure foundation of rock when wise men hear the words of Christ and do them (Matt. 7:24). Living stones founded on Christ are God's spiritual house, God's building (1 Pet. 2:5; 1 Cor. 3:9). They are no more strangers and sojourners, but fellow-citizens with the saints, of the household of God, and "built on the foundation of the apostles and prophets, Christ Jesus himself being the chief cornerstone" (Eph. 2:19,20).

At Corinth the living stones in God's building included Crispus who believed in the Lord and was baptized and many other Corinthians who heard, believed, and were baptized (Acts 18:8; 1 Cor. 1:14). Those in Christ who were reconciled by the cross unto God grew unto a holy temple in the Lord. They were founded on Christ, as are all in Christ, by faith and baptism into his death (see Gal. 3:26,27; Rom. 6:3,4).

An Outline Study Guide

Introduction:

A. Enumerate and discuss what threatens the stability of nations (Prov. 14:34).

_____

B. List and analyze some biblical examples:

Noah _____

Amorites _____

Sodom/Gomorrah _____

Israel/Judah _____

C. Explain the inconsistencies of the "religious right." _____

_____

Rock or Sand:

A. What amazed Jews about the Sermon on the Mount? Provide examples. __

_____

_____

B. How did Jesus conclude the sermon? _____

Who was wise? _____

Foolish? _____

C. What is the sure foundation? _____

Upon This Rock:

A. What question does Jesus raise (Matt. 16:13,16)? _____

How did the population answer? _____

How did Peter answer? _____

B. What did Jesus promise? _____

C. What is the "rock" according to Catholics? _____

D. Respond to Catholic's view of Peter as the rock.

1. Logically: _____

2. Historically: _____

3. Contextually: _____

A Sure Foundation:

A. Show who is the sure foundation (Isa. 28:16; 8:14; Rom. 8:33; Rom. 10:11; 1 Pet. 2:4-8). _____

_____

B. What is meant by Zion in Isaiah 28:16 (Psa. 2:6-9; 110:1,2; Acts 2:33-36; Heb. 12:22-24)? _____

_____

C. Discuss Jesus as the "tried stone" in:

1. Character: _____

2. Will: _____

3. Claim: _____

D. In what sense was Jesus a rejected stone (Psa. 118:22; Matt. 21:33-46; Acts 4:11; 1 Pet. 2:4). _____

_____

E. What does Jesus hold in his hands that assures the church he is the sure foundation (Rev. 1:17,18)? Describe the vision and its message. _____

_____

No Other Foundation:
A. How had Corinthians removed themselves from the sure foundation? _____

_____

B. Discuss Paul's response to this problem (1 Cor. 1:10-13; 3:1-4). _____

_____

C. What foundation did Paul lay there? How (1 Cor. 3:10,11; Acts 18:5,8)?

_____

_____

Conclusion:
A. Summarize how men build on Christ. _____

_____

B. What is formed when men build on the foundation of Christ? _____

_____

Beginning:
In The Last Days

Introduction

Pentecost was a special day for the nation of Israel: the feast of weeks to celebrate the end of the barley harvest and homecoming for tens of thousands of Jews who gathered from all parts of the world; a time to present giant loaves of leavened barley bread to God in thanksgiving for the fruitfulness of the land and to offer sacrifices for the nation; a day to remember bondage to Egypt and to pledge renewed consecration to God (see Exod. 34:22,23; Lev. 23:15-21; Deut. 16:9,10).

Pentecost in A.D. 33 was more than special; it was revolutionary and earth shattering. Fifty days earlier, passover week ended, the barley harvest began, and Jesus of Nazareth broke free from the bonds of death. Ten days before, the resurrected Christ delivered his final words to chosen apostles, reminding them of the coming Spirit and of their world-wide mission (see Mark 16:15,16; Matt. 28:;18-20). "But ye shall receive power, when the Holy Spirit is come upon you: and ye shall be my witnesses both in Jerusalem, and in all Judea and Samaria, and unto the uttermost part of the earth" (Acts 1:8). With these words Jesus departed into the heavens, where he sat down at the right hand of God to begin his rule as Lord and Christ (see Acts 1:9-11; 2:33-36).

The apostles, as ordered by the Lord (see Luke. 24:49), tarried in Jerusalem, awaiting the promised Spirit (see Acts 1:5). "And when the day of Pentecost was now come, they were all together in one place. And suddenly there came from heaven a sound as of the rushing of a mighty wind, and it filled all the house where they were sitting. And there appeared unto them tongues parting asunder, like as of fire; and it sat upon each one of them. And they were all filled with the Holy Spirit, and began to speak with other tongues, as the Spirit gave them utterance" (Acts 2:1-4).

Immersed in the Holy Spirit, the twelve spoke by inspiration and proclaimed for the first time "that God hath made him both Lord and Christ, this Jesus, whom ye crucified" (Acts 2:36). A decade or so later Gentiles received the Spirit, confirming their right to the gospel, and Peter, looking back to that notable Pentecost day, called it *"the beginning"* (Acts 11:15-18).

The Beginning

Pentecost — the beginning. What a fitting day: a day of harvest, a day of celebration, a day of homecoming, a day of thanksgiving, a day of offerings and consecration to God. The harvest of souls began that day — a day of homecoming when men and women returned to God who became their Father in Christ Jesus; a day of celebration and thanksgiving for the blessings of salvation in Christ Jesus; a day of offering and consecrating themselves as spiritual sacrifices to God in Christ Jesus.

Three important events began that day. First, the proclamation of the gospel, the good news of "Jesus Christ and him crucified" (see 1 Cor. 2:2). Peter preached Jesus as: a man approved of God by signs and wonders and mighty powers; a sacrifice and offering delivered up by the determinate counsel and foreknowledge of God; conqueror of death who was not left in Hades and did not see corruption; Lord and Christ exalted above all rule and power (see Acts 2:22-36).

Second, redemption from the bondage of sin was received by Jewish converts. Many Jews heard the gospel preached and were pricked in their hearts; some of them recognized their sinfulness, believed in the Christ, and asked what they should do; they were told to "repent" and "be baptized. . .for the remission of sins"; they that received the truth — about 3000 — were baptized into Christ and into his death (see Acts 2:37-41; Gal. 3:26,27; Rom. 6:3,4).

Third, the new converts banded themselves together into a body committed to Spirit-revealed truth. They continued steadfastly together: walking in the apostles' doctrine; praying; sharing fellowship with one another; breaking bread in memory of the crucified one; and caring for any among them who had need. Thereafter they were called "the church," a body of believers translated out of darkness into light; an assembly of firstborn ones whose names were enrolled in heaven; a company of redeemed ones purchased by the blood of Christ (see Acts 5:11 and 8:1,3; also 1 Pet. 2:9,10; Heb. 12:22,23; Acts 20:;28).

The church began that day in "fact" or "reality," not in conception and plan. Contrary to dispensational thinking, the church embodies and manifests the many faceted wisdom of God — conceived before the foundations of the world "according to the eternal purpose which he purposed in Christ Jesus our Lord" (Eph. 3:10,11). God foreordained both Jews and Gentiles to be "fellow-heirs, and fellow-members of the body, and fellow-partakers of the promise in Christ Jesus through the gospel" (Eph. 3:6-11; see also Eph. 1:3-11; 2:13-18). The church was no afterthought to replace a rejected kingdom. It was central to God's eternal plan and arrived on schedule in fulfillment of prophetic utterances.

The Last Days

The beginning of the church was anticipated in Scripture centuries before the appearance of the Messiah. Isaiah envisioned the establishment of the God's house in the *last days*.

> And it shall come to pass in the latter days, that the mountain of Jehovah's house shall be established on the top of the mountains, and shall be exalted above the hills; and all nations shall flow unto it. And many peoples shall go and say, Come ye, and let us go up to the mountain of Jehovah, to the house of the God of Jacob; and he will teach us of his ways, and we will walk in his paths: for out of Zion shall go forth the law, and the word of Jehovah from Jerusalem (Isa. 2:2,3).

House of God/Church. The prophet Isaiah foresaw the "mountain of Jehovah's house. . .established on the top of the mountains," a reference to the exaltation of God's rule and God's people. He saw all nations flowing into the "house of God," a New Testament description of "the church of the living God" (1 Tim. 3:15; 1 Pet. 2:5; Eph. 2:19).

Jew and Gentile. The prophet likewise saw "all nations," according to God's eternal scheme, flow upward to the mountain of Jehovah's house, "to the house of the God of Jacob." There Jehovah would teach both Jew and Gentile "his ways" and they would "walk in his paths"; there the law would go forth "out of Zion," God's dwelling place and seat of rule; (Psa. 2:6-9; 110:1-5); there his word would come out "from Jerusalem," the heavenly city in which God's people are enrolled and raised to sit with Christ (see Heb. 12:22,23; Eph. 2:6). How fitting that the Lord poured forth his Spirit and revealed his word from the heavens that Pentecost day at literal, earthly Jerusalem and Zion.

Latter Days. Isaiah saw all this coming "to pass in the latter days," a time period precisely defined in the New Testament. Peter associated the "last days" with Pentecost and the manifestation of God's Spirit. "But this is that which hath been spoken through the prophet Joel: And it shall come to pass in the *last days*, saith God" (Acts 2:16,17; see Joel 2:28,29). "Last days" did not mean the final few days before the Lord returns. What Peter called the "beginning" (Acts 11:15) he also called the "last days." And why is this so?

The "last days" described an age, not a few years or days. The "age" of the Messiah, beginning at Pentecost, is the end or final days. The time of the patriarchs and the days of Moses and Israel were past. The law that separated Jew and Gentile and as a tutor brought men to Christ had been abolished, nailed to the cross (Gal. 3:23-25; Eph. 2:14,15; Col. 2:14). At Pentecost the new covenant, dedicated by the blood of Christ, introduced the Messianic age, the "beginning" of a new age which is the "last" age (see Matt. 26:26-28; Heb. 8:6-13; 9:14,15; 12:24).

When the Messiah comes a second time it will be the "last *day*," not "last *days*." All will be raised and gathered for judgment — at the last day (John 5:28,29; 6:40; 12:48; Matt. 25:31-46); the heavens and earth will be dissolved and melted with fervent heat — days will cease (2 Pet. 3:9,10); the saints will

meet the Lord in the air and God's kingdom will be delivered up to the Father
— then comes the end (1 Th. 4:16,17; 1 Cor. 15:24). "Days" or "time" will
end with eternity at the last day when the Lord appears.

The present age of the Messiah is, therefore, the "last days," and is so
defined by New Testament revelation. The first century marked the time God
spoke by his Son at "the end of these days" (ASV) or "in these last days" (NIV)
(Heb. 1:1,2; see Acts 3:22,23). Peter, who called this age the "last days" (Acts
2:16,17), said Christ offered himself as the lamb without spot and blemish at
"the end of the times" (ASV) or "in these last times" (NIV, 1 Pet. 1:18-20).
The Messiah appeared, according to the writer of Hebrews, at "the end of the
ages. . .to put away sin by the sacrifice of himself" (Heb. 9:26). These are the
days Isaiah announced — the days when the Christ would arrive, offer himself
as a sacrifice, and purchase by his blood the church (see Acts 20:28).

The Days of Rome

Daniel also proclaimed the coming of the "latter days" (Dan. 2:28). He
spoke of the church, not as a "house" but a "kingdom," that same body of
people purchased by Christ's blood (Rev. 5:9,10). Daniel's vision came in the
interpretation of a dream seen by King Nebuchadnezzar of Babylon. The king
had seen a man with a head of gold, arms and breasts of silver, belly and thighs
of brass, and legs and feet of iron mixed with clay. The king had also seen a
stone cut out of the mountain that struck the image of the man in the feet and
destroyed it (Dan. 2:31-45).

The interpretation followed a time sequence and identified the "latter days"
with the time of Rome. The head of gold represented Nebuchadnezzar; the arms
and breast portrayed the Medes and Persians, a kingdom that was to "come
after" the king of Babylon; the belly and thighs represented a "third" kingdom,
the Macedonian or Grecian empire which followed the Medes and Persians; the
legs of iron and clay mixed was a "fourth" kingdom, the nation of Rome (Dan.
2:37,39-40).

The stone cut out of the mountain was the indestructible kingdom of God.
The kingdom would come in the "days of those kings," after the rise of the
fourth empire, and would strike the image in the feet, denoting the time of
Rome. Daniel saw what Isaiah saw: the "latter days" arriving in the days of
Rome (Dan. 2:44-45).

Daniel was also looking to the end of the age, to the "latter days," to the
time of the Messianic sacrifice and his purchased kingdom (see Rev. 5:9,10; see
again Heb. 1:1,2; 9:26; 1 Pet. 1:19,20). Another prophecy by Daniel identified
the time of the kingdom with the first appearance of the Messiah, particularly the
ascension of Jesus. The prophet saw one like unto a "son of man" ascend on the
clouds unto the "ancient of days," where he received "dominion, and glory, and
a *kingdom*" (Dan. 7:13,14).

The Ascension
More than 75 times, usually by the Lord himself, the Messianic phrase "son of man" is applied to Jesus. "Who do men say that I the *son of man* am?" Jesus asked (Matt. 16:13). Or, "that ye may know that the *son of man* hath authority on earth to forgive sins. . .I say unto thee, Arise, take up thy bed, and go into the house" (Mark 2:10,11). Daniel, remember, saw one like unto a "son of man" ascending on the clouds to God, where he received a kingdom.

Ten days before Pentecost in the opening of the book of Acts, Luke recorded the ascension of Christ: "And when he had said these things, as they were looking, he was taken up; and a *cloud* received him out of their sight" (Acts 1:9). Peter proclaimed the Lord's destination in his Pentecost sermon: "Being therefore by the right hand of God exalted. . .God hath made him both Lord and Christ, this Jesus whom ye crucified." There, according to two Psalms, during the days of Rome, Jesus became king and began ruling the nations with a rod of iron (Psa. 2:6-9; 110:1-4).

God set his king on his holy hill of Zion and the Psalmist told of the decree: "Thou art my son; This day have I begotten thee" (Psa. 2:7). The New Testament quoted the decree and applied it to the resurrection of Jesus (Acts 13:33; Heb. 1:5; 5:5), from which, as Daniel observed, he received dominion, and power, and glory (see Eph. 1:20-23). The Messiah, according to Psalm 110, was to exercise his rule from the right hand of God by the rod of his strength; a rule as king *and* priest, when he would strike through kings in the day of his wrath. This Psalm referred to Jesus and his present rule as Lord and Christ and as High Priest after the order of Melchizedek (see Matt. 22:44; Acts 2:34-36; Heb. 5:6).

Prophecy looked to the days of Jesus as the age of the Messiah, his reign, his kingdom, his church (see Acts 3:18,24). The resurrection and the ascension brought him to his throne, to the right hand of God, to a position of power and dominion over the uttermost parts of the earth, to his rule as head of the church. This is the time Peter described both as "the beginning" and the "last days."

Conclusion
Jesus himself announced his days in the flesh as the time of prophetic fulfillment. "The time is fulfilled, and the kingdom is at hand" (Mark 1:15). The time proclaimed by the prophets had arrived; it is completed — "fulfilled," the Lord said. These were the "latter days" of Isaiah and Daniel. The kingdom was to come before most of the disciples would die (Mark 9:1).

The kingdom or church could not come during the public ministry of Jesus. The redeemed body of saints, the kingdom, began only after the Lamb of God was slain and "didst purchase unto God with thy blood men of every tribe, and tongue, and people, and nation, and madest them to be unto our God a kingdom" (Rev. 5:9,10); only then could the church be purchased by his blood (Acts

20:28). These are they who have "come unto mount Zion," "unto the city of the living God, the heavenly Jerusalem," "to the general assembly and *church of the firstborn* who are enrolled in heaven," "to God the Judge of all," *"to Jesus the mediator of a new covenant, and to the blood that speaketh better than that of Abel"* — where they received *"a kingdom that cannot be shaken"* (see Heb. 12:22-24,28).

Before Pentecost Jesus anticipated the kingdom and promised to build his church (Mark 1:14,15; Matt. 16:18). After Pentecost Scripture speaks of the reality of both the kingdom and the church (Acts 5:11; 8:1,3; 1 Cor. 1:1,2; Col. 1:13; Heb. 12:28). What happened on that day, when some 3000 men and women obeyed the gospel, marked the "beginning" of the church.

An Outline Study Guide

Introduction:

A. Prepare a brief report on the Jewish Pentecost (Exod. 34:22,23; Lev. 23:15-21; Deut. 16:9,10). _____

_____

B. Discuss a major promise fulfilled on Pentecost A. D. 33. _____

_____

C. What was first proclaimed at Pentecost? What did Peter call this day? ____

_____

The Beginning:

A. What spiritual parallels are found between Jewish Pentecost and A.D. 33. _

_____

B. Discuss the three events that began on Pentecost. _____

_____

C. Where did the church begin in plan and conception (Eph. 3:10,11)? _____

_____

The Last Days:

A. Analyze Isaiah's prophecy of the last days (Isa. 2:2-4). What did the prophet see coming? _____

_____

B. When are the "last days" (Acts 2:16; Heb. 1:1,2; 9:26; 1 Pet. 1:19,20)? _

C. What is the difference between "last days" and "last day"? _____

_____

The Days of Rome:
A. Detail Nebuchadnezzar's dream. _____

_____

_____

B. Explain Daniel's interpretation of each part:

    1. Head: _____

    2. Arms: _____

    3. Belly: _____

    4. Legs: _____

    5. Stone: _____

C. What time frame does the prophecy envision? _____

The Ascension:
A. Explain and interpret Daniel's prophecy of the ascension. To whom does it refer? What was to be received? _____

_____

B. According to Psalm 2:6,7 when would the Messiah rule (see Acts 13:33; Heb. 1:5; 5:5)? _____

_____

C. Where does Psalm 110 portray the Messiah ruling? When was this fulfilled (Acts 2:33-36; Eph. 1:20-23)? _____

_____

Conclusion:
A. What did Jesus teach about the time of the establishment of the kingdom (Mark 1:14,15; 9:1)? _____

_____

B. Why could the church or kingdom not come during Jesus' ministry? _____

C. When is the church or kingdom first seen in reality? _____

Authority:
Head Over the Church

Introduction

The past two centuries have witnessed two extreme ideas concerning the nature of the church. The difference might be framed as — restoration versus modernism. One views the first-century church as a model for all time and insists that each age and each generation must work to restore or maintain the ancient order. The other thinks of the church as a constantly evolving body that must update and modernize itself to meet the challenges of an ever changing society.

"Restoration" says the basic needs of man are always the same and his relationship to God never changes. God in his infinite wisdom, they affirm, knew from eternity the immutable needs of man and planned the church to fill those needs. The pattern, therefore, of the first-century church is forever valid. What man needed in the first century he still needs. The church was and must always be what God willed it to be. To tinker with God's plan is both to impeach the wisdom of God and impose the wisdom of man. The church must conform to God's design, not man's desire.

"Modernism" comes in many varieties, but essentially questions the value of a "static" church. A church of 2000 years ago, they contend, cannot possibly be valid in a modern world. Man must by his own wisdom make judgments as to the best interests of his own generation. Boards, committees, conventions, assemblies, and synods must scrutinize, analyze, and adjust the worship, work, and organization of the church to the perceptions of the present age. The church becomes what the times appear to demand and the church itself thinks. The church is what man desires, not what God designs.

"Authority" in this battle of extremes is the key issue. Authority, of course, is the right to command, to demand, to order — in short, to legislate or pass laws. But who is the authority for the church? That is the question. Is the church its own authority, a self-legislative body that determines its nature and character? Or, is the church subject to a legislative authority outside and beyond itself? Answers depend on two considerations: the relationship of Christ to the church and the nature and extent of biblical authority.

Christ — The Head

Scripture leaves little doubt about the former. Christ's relationship to the church is stated plainly and vividly: God "put all things in subjection under his feet, and gave him to be head over all things to the church, which is his body, the fulness of him that filleth all in all" (Eph. 1:22,23). "And he is the head of the body, the church. . .that in all things he might have the preeminence" (Col. 1:,18). Clearly, as a man's body is subject to its head, so the church is subject to Christ. How could anyone think otherwise? Scripture parallels it to the husband-wife relationship: "For the husband is the head of the wife, as Christ also is the head of the church. . .But as the church is subject to Christ, so let the wives also be to their husbands in everything" (Eph. 5:22,24).

Jesus/God. Some think of this relationship differently because they forget that Jesus is someone special. They regard him as just the best of men. Jesus is that — no doubt! But he is much more. Jesus is God! John said of him: "In the beginning was the Word, and the Word was with God, and the *Word was God*" (John 1:1). At birth Jesus was called "Immanuel," which being interpreted means "God with us" (Matt. 1:23). "In him dwelleth all the fulness of the Godhead bodily" (Col. 2:9).

Jesus/Creator. Jesus was also the creator of all things. "Without him was not anything made that hath been made" (John 1:3). "All things have been created through him. . . and in him all things consist" (Col. 1:16,17). Jesus is an eternal spirit and was present at the beginning. It was he who created man in his own image and likeness (Gen. 1:26).

As God who created all things, including man, Jesus is author and ruler of the creation. He has the prerogative to govern the universe and to direct the steps of man, especially the church of which he is head. "The way of man is not in himself; it is not in man that walketh to direct his steps" (Jer. 10:23). "There is a way which seemeth right unto a man; But the end thereof are the ways of death" (Prov. 14:12).

Jesus/Prophet. Moses recognized the authority of the coming Messiah. The dean of Old Testament prophets declared that God would "raise up a prophet from among their brethren" and, from Jehovah's own lips, "I will put my words in his mouth and he shall speak unto them all that I command him" (Deut. 18:18). The apostle Peter applied this to Jesus (Acts 3:22,23). This confirms what the Hebrew writer said of Jesus as God's Son and God's prophet: "God, having of old time spoken unto the father in the prophets by divers portions and in divers manners, hath at the end of these days spoken unto us in his Son" (Heb. 1:1,2).

Jesus/Lord. It is no mere coincidence that the people most frequently addressed Jesus as "Teacher" and "Lord." In excess of 50 times he is called "Teacher" or "Rabbi" and more than 70 times "Lord." Jesus both recognized and confirmed the legitimacy of those titles. "Ye call me, Teacher, and Lord:

and ye say well; for so I am" (John 13:13). The two terms are compatible because he *taught* the people and did so "as one having *authority*" (Matt. 7:29).

The Sermon on the Mount exemplifies Jesus as a teacher with authority. Again and again he told the people to obey commands because "I say" it. He continually said: "Ye have heard that it was said. . .but *I say* unto you" (Matt. 5:21,21; 27,28; 33,34; 43,44). This astonished the Jews (Matt. 7:29). The scribes taught them to do "this" or "that" because Moses said it, or it was written in Isaiah, or it was a tradition of the elders. But here one says do it because — "I say" so.

Authority belongs to Christ because of who he is — God, Creator, Prophet, and Lord. He himself said to the apostles whom he selected and sent into the world to establish the church: "All authority has been given to me in heaven and on earth" (Matt. 28:18). Jehovah the Father confirmed Jesus' authority in a voice from heaven: "This is my beloved Son, in whom I am well pleased; *Hear ye him*" (Matt. 17:5). The Prophet's message to the church is firm: "And why call ye me, Lord, Lord, and do not the things which I say?" (Luke 6:46). Did his apostles respect and enforce his authority on the church?

Scripture — The Creed

Jesus, of course, never wrote anything that has been preserved. Neither did he choose to reveal his message directly to each man personally. He revealed his will through the writings of selected men unto whom he promised guidance by the Holy Spirit. On his final evening with the apostles when he and they observed the passover feast together, Jesus promised: "These things have I spoken unto you, while yet abiding with you. But the Comforter, even the Holy Spirit, whom the Father will send in my name, he shall teach you all things, and bring to your remembrance all that I said unto you" (John 14:25,26). He also assured them that night: "Howbeit when he, the Spirit of truth, is come, he shall guide you into all truth" (John 16:13).

The Holy Spirit, according to the promise, came to the apostles on the Pentecost after Jesus' resurrection and ascension. The twelve were immersed in the Spirit and spoke by inspiration as the Spirit gave them words (Acts 2:1-4). "We speak God's wisdom in a mystery," Paul later said of the apostles, "even the wisdom that hath been hidden, which God foreordained before the worlds unto our glory"; a wisdom which they spoke — "not in words which man's wisdom teaches, but which the Spirit teacheth" (1 Cor. 2:6,13).

The message was written in understandable words: "How that by revelation was made known unto me the mystery, as I wrote before in few words, whereby, when ye read, ye can perceive my understanding in the mystery of Christ; which in other generations was not made known unto the sons of men, as it hath now been revealed unto his holy apostles and prophets in the Spirit" (Eph. 3:3-5).

These writings were called "scriptures" (2 Pet. 3:15) and were "inspired of

God" (2 Tim. 3:16). "Inspired of God" means the writings were "breathed" or "uttered" by God, so that anyone who reads the "scriptures" is receiving a message from God (see 1 Thess. 2:13). The message is "profitable" and sufficient that "the man of God may be complete, furnished completely unto every good work" (2 Tim. 3:16,17). The Scriptures are "profitable" to — teach, reprove, correct, and instruct in righteousness.

The Scriptures, sometimes called the "oracles of God," an expression which means words or utterances of God (see Rom. 3:1,2), are the standard of both speech and conduct. "If anyone speaks let him speak as the oracles of God" (1 Pet. 4:11). When "ignorant and unsteadfast" men distort or twist the Scriptures, they do it "unto their own destruction" (2 Pet. 3:14-17). Perversion of apostolic writings brings condemnation.

The Galatian epistle declares this truth vividly. Paul marvelled that the churches of Galatia had moved so quickly from the gospel he had preached and they had received. He charged them with believing and obeying another gospel, which is a perversion (Gal. 1:6,7). The problem? They had added circumcision, Jewish feast days, and other aspects of Moses' law to the gospel of Christ. This, he said, is distortion of truth. They had returned to the bondage of the law and thereby severed themselves from Christ and grace (Gal. 4:8-11; 5:1-4).

The apostle spoke plainly: "But though we, or an angel from heaven, should preach unto you any gospel other than that which we preached unto you, let him be anathema. As we have said before, so say I now again, If any man preacheth unto you any gospel other than that which ye received, let him be anathema" (Gal. 1:8,9). He emphatically stated that the church is under apostolic revelation, under the headship of Jesus who revealed these things by the Spirit. This underscores what was taught from the beginning: disciples must continue "steadfastly in the apostles' doctrine" (Acts 2:42).

The apostle John was just as forceful in the three epistles he wrote to condemn and answer Gnostic philosophers. These teachers viewed themselves as elitists who had received special *gnōsis* (knowledge) from God. Their knowledge, they claimed, came to them directly from God. They, accordingly, deluded themselves into believing they had no need of apostles. But in rejecting apostolic revelation they had cut themselves off from God and Christ. So said John. "Whosoever goeth onward and abideth not in the teaching of Christ, hath not God; he that abideth in the teaching, the same hath both the Father and the Son" (2 John 9).

The creed, or "belief," of the church from the beginning has been the Scriptures — the New Testament. Men who replace this or supplement it with "confessions," "catechism," "manuals," "disciplines," "books of prayer," or other human creeds move away from revealed truth — the foundation of the apostles and prophets and Jesus the chief cornerstone (see Eph. 2:20-22; 3:5). Human creeds are nothing more than "traditions of men," a basis for life that both Jesus and the apostles rejected.

A goal of the Pharisees was to bring Jesus and his disciples under "the tradition of the elders." They complained that neither Jesus nor his disciples performed the ceremonial cleansing before meals — "for they wash not their hands before they eat bread" (Matt. 15:1,2). Jesus responded with two points: (1) "And ye have made void the word of God because of your tradition"; (2) "But in vain do they worship me, Teaching as their doctrines the precepts of men" (Matt. 15:1-9). Human traditions tacked onto God's word defile it, distort it, and render it powerless; service or worship based on those traditions is empty and unprofitable.

Paul exposed a similar problem that was shaking the foundations of the church at Colossae. The error he opposed may have been, some scholars suppose, an early form of Gnosticism. Paul argued that the Colossians had received Christ, that he is sufficient, and that they must be rooted and grounded in him (Col. 2:6,7). In him "are all the treasures of wisdom and knowledge hidden"; "in him ye are made full" (Col. 2:4,9). He then warned: "Take heed lest there shall be any one that maketh spoil of you through his philosophy and vain deceit, after the tradition of men, after the rudiments of the world, and not after Christ" (Col. 2:4-10). To be spoiled, captivated by the "tradition of men" is to reject the authority and sufficiency of Christ.

Church — The Body

The church is to Christ "his body" (Eph. 1:22,23). Jesus promised "I will build *my* church," and congregations throughout the world were "churches of Christ" (Matt. 16:18; Rom. 16:16). The term "body" alludes by illustration to the physical body of man and conveys the thought of subjection. A man's body is subject to his head. And since Christ is the head of the body, the body or church must be subject to Christ. No scholar, seminarian, theologian, or any man can define or describe accurately the New Testament church except by reference to the instruction, authority, and headship of Jesus.

What any theologian of his own wisdom perceives the church to be in medieval times, modern times, or the twenty-first century is no guide to what Christ authorized it to be. Christ, the head of the church, designed, built, and gave directions to it in the first century. Since that time he has neither spoken nor written anything new. This in itself indicates its sufficiency as originally planned. If change must be made, if an evolution in nature is necessary, if an updating is required by the times — it is up to the head to give new directions. Otherwise the original design stands.

Conclusion

The remaining chapters of this study are founded on that premise. The name, mission, worship, structure, sufficiency, and purity of the church can be learned from apostolic writings and must be taught and enforced. Those who are interested in the church from a biblical perspective and want to get "back to the Bible" will want to follow subsequent lessons closely.

An Outline Study Guide

Introduction:

A. Identify and discuss two extremes in the past two centuries. _____

_____

B. What important issue does this raise? How? _____

_____

Christ — The Head:

A. Show that Christ is the head of the church (Eph. 1:22,23; Col. 1:18). ____

_____

B. Identify from Scripture that Jesus is God (John 1:1,14; Matt. 1:23). _____

_____

C. As God Jesus was what at the beginning (John 1:3)? What does he derive from this? What is the value of man's wisdom? _____

_____

D. What do the Scriptures say about Jesus as prophet (Deut. 18:15-18; Acts 3:22,23; Heb. 1:1,2)? _____

_____

E. Discuss and illustrate his role as Lord (John 13:13; Matt. 7:29). _____

_____

F. As God, Creator, Prophet, Lord what right does Jesus claim (Matt. 28:18)?

_____

Scripture — The Creed:

A. Rather than writing his own words, what did Jesus promise the apostles (John 14:25,26; 16:13)? _____

B. How or by what means were the apostles accurate and understandable in their writings (Eph. 3:3-5)? _____

C. Define inspiration and demonstrate the sufficiency of Scriptures (2 Tim. 3:16,17; 2 Pet. 3:15,16). _____

D. Describe what happened among the Galatian churches and how Paul reacted to it (Gal. 1:6-9; 4:8-10; 5:1-4). _____

E. To whom did the apostle John respond? Why? What was his message to them (2 John 9-11)? _____

F. How did Jesus react to Pharisaic traditions? What were his conclusions (Matt. 15:1-9)? _____

G. What happened at Colossae and what were Paul's instructions (Col. 2:4-10)?
_____

Church — The Body:
A. Prove that the body is Christ's (Eph. 1:22,23; 5:23-27). _____

_____

B. How could it be argued that the body is sufficient? _____

_____

Conclusion:
A. What is the premise of the remaining lessons? _____

_____

B. Outline the areas of the study that remain. _____

_____

Lesson 7

Membership:
The Fulness of Christ

Introduction

Everyone loves a mystery. They fascinate, they intrigue, they challenge. They excite curiosity and curiosity searches for answers. Some mysteries, however, are unfathomable, unsearchable, past finding out. The universe, including man, is but one example. Every fact scientists dig up about the atom, the cell, or DNA unearths a hundred or a thousand unanswered questions. The mystery goes on and on.

So it is with the mind of God. "O the depth of the wisdom and the knowledge of God! how unsearchable are his judgments, and his ways past tracing out. For who hath known the mind of the Lord? Who hath been his counsellor?" ((Rom. 11:33,34) Scientists, despite advances in biological and physical research, cannot discover the wisdom and thinking of God. What he prepared for mankind, eyes had not seen, ears had not heard, and had never entered the heart of any man (1 Cor. 2:9). It was a "mystery which for ages hath been hid in God who created all things" (Eph. 3:9).

But man need not despair: "for the Spirit searcheth all things, yea, the deep things of God" (1 Cor. 2:11). The Holy Spirit explored the mind of God and revealed his mystery "unto his holy apostles and prophets" (Eph. 3:5). Apostles and prophets spoke God's "wisdom in a mystery, even the wisdom that hath been hidden, which God foreordained before the worlds unto our glory" (1 Cor. 2:7). They also recorded the mystery in Scripture that men who read it can understand God's purpose in Christ Jesus through the gospel (Eph. 3:3,4; 2 Tim. 3:16,17).

That revealed gospel is the mystery made known: an unveiling of God's "eternal purpose which he purposed in Christ Jesus," an uncovering of the "unsearchable riches of Christ," and an unfolding of the church as "the fulness of him [Christ] that filleth all in all" (Eph. 3:8-11; 1:22,23).

The Ephesian letter is Paul's grand treatise on the church. There the apostle outlined the glorious scheme of human redemption hidden in the mind of God from eternity and manifested at the fullness of the times in Christ Jesus. There he saw the church as an eternally planned, divinely crafted body of believers at peace with God. The first two chapters of the epistle highlight the church as the fullness of Christ, the workmanship of God, and the habitation of God in the Spirit.

Fullness of Christ

Chapter one stresses the church as the body of Christ, "the fulness of him that filleth all in all" (Eph. 1:22,23). "Fulness" suggests completeness or sufficiency. Christ himself is sufficient — "for in him dwelleth all the fulness of the Godhead bodily" and in him "are all the treasures of wisdom and knowledge hidden" (Col. 2:9). The church is sufficient — for "in him [Christ] ye are made full" (Col. 2:10). The church, because it is in Christ and because it is the body of Christ, receives all spiritual blessings. Jesus fills "all" in the body with "all things." But this is to get ahead of the story.

Paul's essay begins appropriately with an expression of praise to God: "Blessed be the God and Father of our Lord Jesus Christ, who hath blessed us with every spiritual blessing in heavenly places in Christ" (Eph. 1:3). Paul's opening is clear: Praise God from whom all blessings flow (1:6,12,14); Honor him who provides "every spiritual blessing" to his people (1:22,23); Glorify the One who supplies all things "in heavenly places" to those in Christ (1:4,5,6,7,9,10, 11).

God's blessings originated in his choice — "even as he chose us in him before the foundation of the world, that we should be holy and without blemish before him in love" (Eph. 1:4). The selection was not individual, arbitrary, or based on man's goodness. The scheme centered in Christ, his coming, his death, and the call of men to faith by the gospel. God "chose you from the beginning unto salvation in sanctification of the Spirit and belief of the truth; *whereunto he called you through the gospel*" (2 Thess. 2:13,14). God's call by the gospel, man's response to the good news, and man's entrance into Christ form "an elect race, a royal priesthood, a holy nation, *a people for God's own possession*" (1 Pet. 2:9; see Eph. 1:14).

The chosen race are they whom he foreordained "unto adoption as sons through Jesus Christ unto himself, according to the good pleasure of his will" (Eph. 1:5). When men by faith are baptized into Christ, they put on Christ and become sons of God (Gal. 3:26,27). God's predetermined will and good pleasure arranged for man's adoption unto himself "through Christ" — not by respect of persons in predestination of individuals. In Christ man is elevated from a bondservant of sin to privilege in God's family as a son (see Rom. 8:14-17; John 8:31-35).

The blessing of sonship comes by "his grace, which he freely bestowed on us in the Beloved: in whom we have our redemption through his blood, the forgiveness of our trespasses, according to the riches of his grace" (Eph. 1:6,7). Forgiveness that redeems man from the bondage of Satan is God's free gift of grace, but is granted only to those "in the Beloved. . .through his blood."

Again, the gospel calls man to faith by which he is baptized into Christ and into his death, where the blood was shed (Rom. 6:3; see Gal. 3:26,27).

Outside Christ God provides no spiritual blessings. His foreordained purpose was "to sum up all things in Christ, the things in the heavens, and the things upon the earth" (Eph. 1:10). The blessings of heaven — God's grace and will and purpose — are gathered together in Christ with God's earthly creature of sin — man and his transgressions. There, according to God's plan, man's sins are absolved, he becomes God's "heritage," God's own possession, and is filled with all things (Eph. 1:11-14,22,23).

Workmanship of God

Chapter two opens with a portrait of God's transforming work of grace: how God lifted man from the pit of sin, elevated him unto Christ to heavenly places, and crafted and created him in Jesus unto a foreordained life of good works (Eph. 2:1-10). Man is viewed as a subject of sin, an object of grace, and a project of design.

Man before grace is spiritually "dead through your trespasses and sins," a condition that creates enmity between him and God and alienates him from the blessings of heaven (see Isa. 59:1,2; Jas. 4:4; Col. 1:21). All had become "by nature children of wrath," doomed to the eternal vengeance of God (see 2 Thess. 1:7-9; Rev. 21:8); not sinners by birth, as the context shows, but by "a mode of feeling and acting which by long habit [had] become nature" (*Greek-English Lexicon of the New Testament*, Joseph Henry Thayer 660). They had "walked according to the course of this world, according to the prince of the powers of the air, of the spirit that now worketh in the sons of disobedience" (v. 2). They had "lived in the lusts of [their] flesh, doing the desires of the flesh and of the mind" (v. 3).

God by grace raised them from spiritual death. Merciful, loving, and gracious, he made them alive in Christ Jesus (vv. 4,5). Raised to fellowship with Christ, they sat with him in heavenly places and enjoyed the riches of God's grace and kindness toward them in Christ Jesus (vv. 6,7). "For by grace have ye been saved through faith; and that not of yourselves, it is the gift of God; not of works, that no man should glory" (v. 8).

Men by grace become God's "workmanship," a project of his design and a product of his craftmanship (v. 10). As creation shows God's handiwork and a vessel manifests the artistry of the potter, so new men in Christ display the creative work of God's power in the hearts of sinners. Men once devoted to evil works are "created in Christ Jesus for good works, which God afore prepared that we should walk in them" (v. 10).

God's transforming power to remake and recreate man into the image of his Son comes by the Spirit through the gospel. That was apparent at Pentecost, when the church began. There the apostles received power from on high by baptism in the Spirit and spoke as the Spirit gave them utterance (see Luke 24:49; Acts 1:5,8; 2:1-4). Thousands of Jews heard the Spirit-filled gospel, and about 3000 of them were pricked in their hearts, received the word, were baptized, and continued steadfastly in the apostles' doctrine (Acts 2:1-4,37-42). Begotten by the gospel, the word of truth, they were born anew by the water and the Spirit when the Spirit's message moved them to baptism into Christ and his death (see 1 Cor. 4:15; Jas. 1:18; 1 Pet. 1:22,23; John 3:3-5; Rom. 6:3). Out of baptism they arose "new creatures" in Christ to walk in newness of life (see Rom. 6:3,4; 2 Cor. 5:17).

Jesus illustrated man's renewal in the parable of the sower. The seed is the word of God. Fertile soil is a honest and good heart. Seed is sown in good soil, dies, sprouts, yields a new plant, and produces fruit. So the word takes root in receptive minds, transforms itself into spiritual life, and produces fruit of the Spirit — the fruit of love, joy, peace, longsuffering, kindness, goodness, faithfulness, meekness, self-control (see Luke 8:11-15; Gal. 5:22,23). The result? A "new man, that after God is created in righteousness and holiness of truth" (Eph. 4:24). But how specifically does God's Spirit by the gospel transform man into a new creature that he might be added to the church?

Hearing. Hearing and understanding the message of the gospel is the beginning of salvation in Christ. Jews remain to this day hardened in unbelief because in their hearing they do not understand and receive the gospel lest they should perceive, hear, understand, turn, and Christ should heal them (Matt. 13:13-15). Men cannot believe and call on the Lord for salvation until they hear the gospel (Rom. 10:9-17). Conversion of some 3000 began on Pentecost when "they heard" (Acts 2:37); so it was at Samaria (Acts 8:6), Philippi (Acts 16:14), and Corinth (Acts 18:8).

Faith/Confession. What men hear they must believe and confess. "So belief cometh of hearing, and hearing by the word of Christ" (Rom. 10:17). "For with the heart man believeth unto righteousness; and with the mouth confession is made unto salvation" (Rom. 10:9,10). When the ideas, truths, principles, and message of the gospel fill the mind and take root in the soul, they convict sinners that God is, that Jesus is his Son, and that the good news of salvation is the word of God (Heb. 11:6; John 20:30,31; 1 Thess 2:13). They, like Abel and Noah and Abraham, are assured of things hoped for, convicted of things not seen, and moved to obedience (Heb. 11:1,4,7,8). Salvation, entrance into Christ, membership in the body were never by faith alone. These blessings came by "obedience of faith," as Paul expressed it in his epistle on justification by faith (Rom. 1:5; 16:26). Faith that works, faith that obeys; this is the faith that transforms, that justifies, and that saves (Jas. 2:22-24; Heb. 5:8,9; Matt. 7:21,22); not by perfection of works alone, as the same apostle cogently argued in that same letter (Rom. 4:1-8).

Repentance. The "obedience of faith" begins with repentance. When John the Baptist and Jesus announced the coming kingdom, they called on men to repent (Matt. 3:1,2; Mark 1:14,15). Jesus said later: "I tell you, Nay: but, except you repent, ye shall all in like manner perish" (Lk. 13:3). Repentance was to be preached to all nations beginning at Jerusalem, where they of Israel heard the apostle Peter command, "Repent ye" (Lk. 24:47; Acts 2:38). God commands "men that they should all everywhere repent" (Acts 17:30). Repentance is that transformed mind that yields a transformed life. Penitent believers cease the practice of sin — drunks no longer drink, thieves no longer steal, and fornicators no longer fornicate.

Baptism. Man's new knowledge (hearing), new conviction (faith), and new behavior (repentance), regardless of his sincerity, do not wash away sins, cleanse the soul, or put him into Christ. He must, as Saul of Tarsus, arise and be baptized to wash away his sins (Acts 22:16). He must repent and "be baptized. . .unto the remission of sins" (Acts 2:38). Baptism earns nothing. It puts one into Christ, into his death, and into the church (Gal. 3:26,27; Rom. 6:3,4; 1 Cor. 12:13; see Acts 2:47). Baptism, the expression of a penitent believer, doth save; it is the sinner's call and plea to God for a good conscience (1 Pet. 1:21; Acts 22:16).

Habitation of the Spirit

Chapter 2 concludes with a description of God's church as a "habitation of God in the Spirit" (Eph. 2:22). Jehovah, the infinite, eternal one and Lord of heaven and earth, dwells not in temples made with hands (Acts 17:24). The Holy One, according to his purpose in Christ Jesus, crafted for himself a spiritual dwelling in heavenly places — the realm of the redeemed, reconciled, purified body of Christ, the church (Eph. 2:11-22).

There he unites hostile elements — "so making peace" (Eph. 2:15). Gentiles, once a far off, were by the blood of Christ brought near to God. The law of Moses, a barrier between Jew and Gentile, was abrogated and the two under the new covenant were created into "one new man" in Christ (Eph. 2:15). There men of every tribe and tongue and people and nation are redeemed and reconciled to one another (see Rev. 5:9,10). Jew and Gentile, bond and free, male and female, black and white, young and old are united, equal, and of the same mind and soul (see Gal. 3:26-29; 1 Cor. 1:10; Phil. 2:2-4).

They all "have. . .access in one Spirit unto the Father" (Eph. 2:18). The gospel of peace was preached "to you that were afar off" (Gentiles) and "to them that were nigh" (Jews). So it must be to "every creature" and "all the nations" (Mark 16:15; Matt. 28:19). They in Christ, redeemed and reconciled, are "no more strangers and sojourners, but ye are fellow-citizens of the saints, and of the household of God" (Eph. 2:19). Response to the gospel in obedient belief not only raises men to sit with Christ in heavenly places (Eph. 2:6), but elevates them to the status of citizens, consecrates them to lives of sainthood, and exalts them to the privilege of sonship.

There men's lives are founded on the revelation of the Spirit, "being built on the foundation of the apostles and prophets, Christ Jesus himself being the chief cornerstone" (Eph. 2:20; 3:5). The basis of life is no longer the "desires of the flesh and of the mind"; all of that has been crucified with the old man of sins and, as Paul said of himself, "it is no longer I that live, but Christ liveth in me" (see Eph. 2:1-3; Gal. 2:20). In Christ the old man of lust is "put to death," "put off," and "put away" and the new man of holiness is "put on" (see Col. 2:5,9,10,12; Eph. 4:22-24). The mind and the affections are now set on things above, where Christ is seated at God's right hand and where citizenship is heavenly and spiritual (see Col. 3:1,2; Phil. 3:20).

There every man in Christ is a "building" and they all "fitly framed together, groweth into a holy temple in the Lord, in whom they are builded together for a habitation of God in the Spirit" (Eph. 2:21,22). Redeemed by the blood of Christ and reconciled unto God by the cross, the church becomes the hallowed sanctuary where God dwells. He abides in them and they abide in him (1 John 4:16).

There in that most holy place appears the effulgence and brightness of God's glory, manifested in the radiant beauty of his Son and reflected in the lives of purified saints who by grace are conformed to the image of the Son's likeness (see John 1:14; Heb. 1:3; Rom. 8:29). There divine services are offered to God by a "holy priesthood" that offers "up spiritual sacrifices, acceptable to God, through Jesus Christ" (see 1 Pet. 2:5).

The church is the restored tabernacle of David, a spiritual temple honored by the presence of God (see Acts 15:13-21). Men must approach it with reverence and awe, coming with something to offer. Jesus offered himself and requires no less of any who enter its portals and take their place within its sacred walls. "I beseech you therefore, brethren, by the mercies of God, to present your bodies a living sacrifice, holy, acceptable to God, which is your spiritual service" (Rom. 12:1).

Conclusion

Bring Christ your broken life
So marred by sin
He will create anew,
Make whole again;
Your empty, wasted years
He will restore,
And your iniquities
Remember no more.

by T. O. Chisholm

An Outline Study Guide

Introduction:

A. Identify and discuss two mysteries that are unfathomable. _____

_____

B. How is the mystery of God's mind solved (1 Cor. 2:11; Eph. 3:3-5)? _____

_____

C. What is unveiled in the uncovering of the mystery (Eph. 3:8-11; 1:22,23)?

_____

Fullness of Christ:

A. What does fullness mean? _____

Of what is Christ full? The church (Col. 2:9,10; Eph. 1:22,23)? _____

_____

B. To whom do Christians owe praise (Eph. 1:3)? Why? _____

_____

C. How has God chosen Christians (Eph. 1:4)? Where? _____

_____

D. How are the chosen made sons (Eph. 1:5,6)? Where? _____

_____

E. What is summed up in Christ (Eph. 1:10,11)? _____

_____

Workmanship of God:

A. What is man's condition by nature (Eph. 2:1-3)? What does nature mean

here? _____

_____

B. How is man raised up from spiritual death (Eph. 2:4-9)? It is not by what?

_____

C. What does "workmanship" mean? _____

D. Detail the process by which man is transformed (Acts 2; Luke 8:11-15). __

_____

E. Specify and explain the actual steps of this transformation (Acts 2:37; Rom. 10:9,10,17; Acts 2:38). _____

_____

Habitation of the Spirit:
A. Where does God not dwell (Acts 17:24)? _____

What did he craft for his dwelling place (Eph. 2:19-22)? _____

B. Who was united in one body (Eph. 2:11-16)? To whom would this apply today (Gal. 3:28)? _____

_____

C. To whom do men in Christ have access (Eph. 2:18)?   They are no longer what (Eph. 2:19)? _____

_____

D. What are men in Christ founded on (Eph. 2:20)? What does this refer to?

_____

_____

E. As a habitation of the Spirit what must men put away (Col. 3:5,9,10,12; Eph. 4:22-24)? _____

_____

F. As a holy priesthood what do Christians offer (1 Pet. 2:5; Rom. 12:1)? __

_____

Conclusion: Relate the hymn "Bring Christ Your Broken Life" to the point of the lesson.

Name:
Is Christ Divided?

Introduction

And Moses said unto God, Behold, when I come unto the children of Israel, and shall say unto them, The God of your fathers hath sent me unto you; and they shall say to me, What is his name? What shall I say unto them? And God said unto Moses, I AM THAT I AM: and he said, Thus shalt thou say unto the children of Israel, I AM hath sent me unto you. And God said moreover unto Moses, Thus shalt thou say unto the children of Israel, Jehovah, The God of Abraham, the God of Isaac, and the God of Jacob, hath sent me unto you: this is my name for ever, and this is my memorial unto all generations (Exod. 3:13-15).

The above conversation transpired between Jehovah and Moses at the burning bush. God had called Moses from the flocks of his father-in-law to deliver Israel from Egyptian bondage and the humble shepherd was both skeptical and reluctant. He needed assurance. How were God's people to know who Moses was and who had sent him?

God's response to Moses highlights three important thoughts about names. First, names have meaning and significance. The name Jehovah, meaning "I AM," declares the "real, perfect, unconditioned, independent existence" of God (*Pulpit Commentary*). It says God is the eternal, uncaused, infinite One. Names, secondly, signify relationships. The name "Jehovah" meant nothing to many nations, but it tells Israel that it is their God, the God of their fathers, that has sent Moses. Finally, names are a memorial to identity and character. Jehovah is God's name forever and will, as a memorial unto all generations, identify him and his presence with Israel.

No perceptive Bible student can read Scripture without being impressed with the significance of names. Abram's name was changed to Abraham, "father of a multitude," when God promised through his seed to bless all families of the earth (Gen. 17:4,5). Jacob's name became "Israel" — "to strive with God" — after he wrestled with Jehovah and prevailed (Gen. 32:28). "Bethel" and

"Ebenezer" are only two of hundreds of meaningful names that memorialized and honored special places and events of Bible history (see Gen 28:19 and 1 Sam. 7:12). The New Testament follows and emphasizes this pattern also.

When the "Word" became flesh and dwelt among men, the angel named him "Jesus" — "for he shall save the people from their sins" (Matt. 1:21). Christians honor that name, confess it, are baptized into it, and call him "savior," knowing that there is no "other name under heaven, that is given among men, wherein we must be saved" (Acts 4:12).

Denominational Names

Surprisingly, in view of the biblical precedent, denominationalists affirm that — "there is nothing in a name" and "a rose by any other name is still a rose." This they often say in support of sectarian names like "Baptist," "Presbyterian," "Methodist," "Episcopalian," "Pentecostal," "Lutheran," "Wesleyan," etc. They admit such names are not biblical, but contend that each stands for a biblical concept which they as a body stress.

Paradoxically, there is *something* in a name and these designations mean everything when defense of sectarian viewpoints is necessary. A "Presbyterian" surely will not be called a "Baptist." God forbid! That name implies "immersion" and he believes in "sprinkling." And a "Baptist" will not accept the name "Episcopalian," since that name describes an organization of diocesan "bishops" who rule many congregations and he believes in a "congregational" form of church government. Suddenly, names are significant and a church by some other name is offended. Why, one wonders, is God not offended by names he never authorized — names that honor sectarian practices and concepts?

"Sectarianism" is the key word. That is the problem. Modern religious names are promulgated and propagated out of a false understanding of the New Testament church. Denominationalists, especially since the Reformation, view the "one body" as a universal church consisting of a multiplicity of different churches. To them, Christ is the vine and the branches are individual denominational bodies (see John 15:1-6). This position ignores the context of Jesus words. Here Jesus spoke to his disciples. He talked with them about their relationship to him and their need to bear fruit in their lives. The church was yet future and is not even anticipated here. The church universal is not the vine. Jesus is the vine. The branches are not denominational bodies. The disciples are the branches.

The church universal consists not of local churches but of all Christians whose names are enrolled in heaven (Heb. 12:22,23). Local churches sometimes include erring disciples whom God has blotted out of the book of life. Or, churches occasionally go so far into apostasy that God removes their lampstand (see Rev. 2:5). Justification of denominationalism and all its sectarian names has no basis in Scripture.

Origin of Denominationalism

Denominationalism traces its origin to two causes: carnality and faith alone. At times ambitious men in arrogance and strife and carnality promote themselves above the Lord. Or, followers exalt these leaders and champion their concepts beyond what is written. Modern denominationalism also finds its roots in "faith only," the fatal flaw of the Reformation and the dominant view of sectarian theologians. Both carnality and faith alone are open violations of New Testament teaching.

Carnality. Carnality plagued the church at Corinth and fostered sectarianism. The "wisdom of the world" was more important than the "word of the cross." "Christ and him crucified" had taken a back seat to a "carnal" spirit (1 Cor. 1:17-25; 3:1-4). Brethren there were saying, "I am of Paul," "I of Apollos," "I of Cephas," and "I of Christ." Sectarian groups formed because they were "carnal," because they were "babes in Christ." "Jealousy and strife" prevailed and they walked "after the manner of men" (1 Cor. 3:1-4).

The apostle replied to their sectarianism in two ways. First, he emphasized the oneness, sameness, unity that must adhere among brethren in Christ. "Now I beseech you, brethren, through the name of our Lord Jesus Christ, that ye all speak the same thing, and that there be no divisions among you; but that ye be perfected together in the same mind and in the same judgment" (1 Cor. 1:10). Second, he asked a series of revealing questions. "Is Christ divided? Was Paul crucified for you? or were you baptized into the name of Paul?" (1 Cor. 1:12,13) With a sense of relief he thanked God he had baptized none of them except Crispus and Gaius.

Sectarianism in every age must ponder these questions. Must not all in Christ be one? Must not sameness and unity abound among all who confess Jesus? Is there not but one body, one Spirit, one hope, one Lord, one faith, one baptism, and one God (Eph. 4:4-6)? Was Luther or Calvin crucified for you? Were you baptized into the name of Wesley or Asbury? And, might it be added, is there nothing at all in a name?

Faith Only. Diverse and warring factions among today's denominational bodies manifest the same carnal spirit, but find their origin in the Augustinian/Lutheran/Calvinistic idea of — "faith only." Once men believed salvation comes by "faith only" — nothing else really mattered. It made no difference what name bodies wore and exalted, how members were baptized or admitted to the group, what form of worship they offered, what activities the denomination supported, or how it was structurally organized. Sectarian denominationalism is but a symptom of the theological error that faith alone is sufficient.

Only when religious leaders understand that, like Abraham, men are justified by "obedience of faith" will they take seriously what God authorized his body to be or do (see Rom. 1:5; 16:26; Jas. 2:22-24; Heb. 11:1-8). When Jesus actually becomes "Lord" to men, as all must confess, then they will grasp the need to do the will of the Father (see Rom. 10:9,10; Matt. 7:21,22; Luke 6:46). When denominational churches assent to both the necessity and sufficiency of the gospel, they will see the importance of name, organization, worship, work, membership, and all truths regarding the character of the first-century church. What then does the Bible teach disciples about the name of God and Christ?

Name of God and Christ

Does the church have a name? That question has been fodder for much discussion and many debates. Some may have argued that the church had a specific name and any deviation from it is heresy. Others contend that names are unimportant and only the character of the church matters. Each of these views is extreme.

What, then, is the answer? One, the church belongs to God and Christ. It is an eternal creation of God; it is his family or household, his temple or dwelling place, and his kingdom or domain of rule (Eph. 3:10,11; 2:19; 1 Cor. 3:16,17; Acts 8:12). Additionally, the church was built by Christ; he is its head, redeemer, savior, husband, king, and lawgiver (Matt. 16:18; Eph. 1:22,23; Acts 20:28; Eph. 5:23-25; Col. 1:13; Jas. 4:11,12). One would therefore expect the church in name to be related to God and Christ. And that is precisely what is found in the Bible.

The Scriptures speak of the "church of God," the "churches of God," the "church of Thessalonians in God," and the "churches of God which are in Judea in Christ Jesus" (1 Cor. 1:2; 2 Thess. 1:4; 1 Thess. 1:1; 2:14). The New Testament likewise speaks of the "church of the Lord," "churches of Christ," "churches of Judea in Christ," and, again, "churches of God which are in Judea in Christ Jesus" (Acts 20:28; Rom. 16:16; Gal. 1:22; 1 Thess. 2:14).

Used more often than any of these expressions is simply "the church." The first century was not abundantly plagued with denominational sectarianism and knew only one church. They would then speak of "the church" in Cenchrea, Ephesus, Smyrna, or Laodicea (Rom. 16:1; Rev. 2:1,8; 3:14). Or, they spoke of many churches in a region as "the churches" of Galatia, Macedonia, or Asia (Gal. 1:2; 2 Cor. 8:1; Rev. 1:4).

The church had no official name. The church at the outset was not known exclusively as "the church," "the church of God," or "the church of Christ." Any or all of those designations are scriptural and accurate names for the church to wear, but none is "the name."

Does this justify assuming that the "name" of the church is unimportant and that "there is nothing in a name"? Names have meanings, express ideas, and are necessary to denote people, places, and things. God's people must be called something, New Testament writers knew that, and gave them such descriptions as already outlined.

Those who seek to get "back to the Bible" and to the first-century practices will be content with biblical designations. They recognize the need to bring glory to *God* in the church and to glorify *God* in the name of Christ. "Now unto him that is able to do exceeding abundantly above all that we ask or think, according to the power that worketh in us, *unto him be the glory* in the church and in Christ Jesus unto all generations for ever and ever, Amen" (Eph. 3:20,21).

So it is with the name of Christ. Christ was honored by the very name God gave the disciples. "And it came to pass, that even for a whole year they were gathered together with the church, and taught much people; and that the disciples were called *Christians* first in Antioch" (Acts 11:26). The word for "called," as elsewhere in the New Testament, refers to a "Divine" call (Matt. 2:12,22; Luke 2:22; Acts 10:22; Rom. 7:3 Heb. 8:5; 11:7; 12:25) — hence a name which God gave. Peter exalted the name of Christ when he exhorted brethren: "But if a man suffer as a Christian, let him not be ashamed; but let him *glorify God in this name*" (1 Pet. 4:16).

Conclusion

Why then do religious groups take seriously names, except when it involves giving honor and glory to God and Christ? None of them would accept the name "Church of Satan" or "The Gay Church" because of what those names mean and what they say. Why do they honor designations that exalt human traditions and foster carnality and division? True, merely wearing the name "Christian," "church of God," or "church of Christ" will not make an individual or a church these things. On the other hand, if this is what a person or church is, why not call it that? It surely makes no sense to go beyond Scripture and invent names that are divisive and harmful. Why not glorify God and Christ by exalting their names?

An Outline Study Guide

Introduction:

A. Discuss Jehovah's conversation with Moses. What three things are learned

about names? _____

_____

B. What are some Bible names that stress the significance of names and what

do these names mean? _____

_____

C. What is the significance of the name "Jesus" (Matt. 1:21; Acts 4:12)? ____

_____

Denominational Names:

A. How do denominationalists argue the insignificance of names? _____

_____

B. Show how they believe there is *something* in a name. _____

_____

C. Explore the denominational concept of the universal church. What is wrong
   with the idea (John 15:1-8; Heb. 12:22,23; Rev. 2:5)? _____

_____

Origin of Denominationalism:

A. What is the origin of denominationalism? Name two. _____

_____

B. Discuss "carnality." What did it cause at Corinth (1 Cor. 3:1-4)? _____
   _____ How did Paul respond to this
   condition (1 Cor. 1:10-13)? _____
   How could Paul's questions be framed today? _____

_____

C. Why does "faith only" produce sectarianism? _____
   _____ What does the Bible say about "faith
   only" (Rom. 1:5; 16:26; Jas. 2:22-24; Heb. 11:1-8)? _____

_____

Name of God and Christ:

A: How is the church related to God (Eph. 3:10,11; 2:19; 1 Cor. 3:16,17; Acts
   8:12)? _____
   To Christ (Matt. 16:18; Eph. 1:22,23; Acts 20:28; Eph. 5:23-25; Col. 1:13;
   Jas. 4:11,12)? _____

B. List names of the church related to God (1 Cor. 1:2; 1 Thess. 2:14). _____

_____

   To Christ (Acts 20:28; Rom. 16:16; Gal. 1:22; 1 Thess. 2:14). _____

C. Does the church have an official name? If yes, show why. _____

   If no, does this justify just any name? _____

D. Who is the church to glorify (Eph. 3:21)? _____

   Did God give disciples a name by which to glorify Christ (Acts 11:26; 1 Pet.

   4:16)? _____

   Examine the word "called" in Acts 11:26. _____

   _____

Conclusion:

A. Do denominationalists really believe there is nothing in a name? _____

   _____

B. Does wearing the name of "Christ" make one a Christian? _____

   _____

C. What do sectarian names foster? _____

   _____

Organization:
Elders in Every Church

Introduction

The church in its universal sense is the "general assembly" of saints "who are enrolled in heaven" (see Heb. 12:23). This body of believers is a living entity animated and sustained spiritually by the life-giving blood of Jesus (see Acts 20:28). It is a spiritual "organism," not an "organization" or "institution." As a world-wide body of men and women in Christ, it has no earthly structure. It is a body of many members under the direct control of Christ as head and functions distributively as each member serves individually.

The church, however, functions as a unit on a different level — as a local church. When the church was built on the foundation of the apostles and prophets in each community, it was assigned specific functions as a group. On this level it functioned as a team. No group can work as a unit without some method of operation, whether called "systematic arrangement" or "organization." Even the physical body — an organism — has system or organization in the way it functions. The local church, unlike the universal church, is not merely individuals working.

The church at Corinth, at Philippi, or at Ephesus assembled, for example. They also fulfilled the mission of evangelism, edification, benevolence, and discipline. To accomplish these purposes the church needed structure and that structure was "congregational" with each local church being equal, independent, and self-governing. Getting back to the Bible demands an appreciation, understanding, and respect for a system of local control. Two important passages set the stage for a study of the organization of the Lord's church.

And he gave some to be *apostles*; and some, *prophets*; and some *evangelists*; and some, *pastors* and *teachers* (Eph. 4:11).

Paul and Timothy, servants of Christ Jesus, to all the saints in Christ Jesus that are at Philippi, with the *bishops* and *deacons* (Phil. 1:1).

Apostles and Prophets. Jesus gave some brethren the gifts to be apostles and prophets. The role of these men bore at times a relationship to local churches, but as a whole was more broadly based. Their work involved primarily the revealing of truth. God by revelation made known the "mystery of Christ," the gospel, which apostles both spoke and wrote. Paul said the gospel was "revealed unto holy apostles and prophets in the Spirit" (see Eph. 3:1-6). When truth was completely revealed and confirmed by signs that followed (Mark 16:17-20; 2 Tim. 3:16,17; Jude 3), the work of apostles and prophets ceased (see 1 Cor. 13:8-10). They were ministers of the new covenant and their message became the foundation on which the church was built (2 Cor. 3:3-6; Eph. 2:19-22). Every local church, whether at Jerusalem, Antioch, or Rome, was founded on "apostles and prophets, Christ Jesus himself being the chief cornerstone" (Eph. 2:20; see 1 Cor. 3:10,11). The message of apostles and prophets governed local churches and is with them today as a foundation, but other men were responsible for the systematic function of those bodies.

Elders

Bishops/Pastors/Elders. The Bible first mentions "elders" in the church when a famine came to Judea. The funds and goods given by other brethren to assist those needy churches was sent "to the elders by the hand of Barnabas and Saul" (Acts 11:30). Their work as overseers is only hinted at here. The next reference to elders is the appointments made by the apostle Paul on his first preaching tour. After establishing churches in several communities of Asia Minor the apostle returned to each and "appointed for them elders in every church" (Acts 14:23). Looking at the work attributed to them elsewhere, it is evident these men were the leaders in local churches. But who and what are these men who are called — "elders"?

Paul spoke to this question on his third preaching tour when he called a group of elders to meet him on the island of Miletus. There he instructed them about their role (see Acts 20:17). "Take heed unto yourselves, and to all the flock, in which the Holy Spirit hath made you *bishops*, to *feed* the church of the Lord which he purchased with his own blood" (Acts 20:28).

The church is viewed as a "flock" of sheep, and elders ("presbyters" from Greek, *presbuteros*) have the general responsibility to "take heed" or "guard" (NIV) the flock; to "consider," "attend to," and "take care of" the members (see *Harpers Analytical Lexicon*). They had been appointed "bishops" or "overseers" (NIV), a term meaning "to look upon" or "inspect" (*epi* = "upon" + *skopos* = "seeing"). Elders and bishops were the same men in New Testament times and the word "bishop" denotes the role to "watch in behalf of your souls" (Heb. 13:17). He also told them to "feed" or "shepherd" (NIV) the church, using the verb form of the word for "shepherd" or "pastor" (*poimainō*). Elders and pastors were also the same men in the first century. Elders as shepherds are to see that the sheep are fed, tended, and protected.

Peter also used forms of these three terms to describe the overseers of the church. "The *elders* therefore among you I exhort. . . *tend* the flock of God which is among you, exercising the *oversight*" (1 Pet. 5:1,2). Elders, again, are told to "tend," verb form of the term shepherd or pastor, and exercise "oversight," a participial form of the word bishop or overseer. The oversight of elders is limited to "the flock of God which is among you" — the local church in which they were appointed (see again Acts 14:23). Elders' work in the local church is to build on the foundation truths revealed by apostles and prophets.

Elders/Presbyters, Pastors/Shepherds, and Bishops/Overseers are six terms used by biblical writers to define the leaders of a local church. The word "elder" signifies age, maturity, wisdom. This is apparent from the list of qualifications they must meet — married, having believing children, ruling well their own house, not a novice, without reproach, blameless, not contentious, no brawler, not soon angry, soberminded, apt to teach, gentle, holy, etc. (see 1 Tim. 3:1-7 and Tit. 1:5-9).

"Bishop" or "overseer" highlights the function of "rule" or "leadership." As a father rules his household, including both basic and incidental decisions, so bishops rule the church (see 1 Tim. 3:5). Faithful bishops observe the needs of God's spiritual family and "take care" of those needs as they would their own families. Bishops must be respected watchmen who lead the flock by example and moral suasion, not as lords and despots (1 Pet. 5:3). Each member will then "obey" and "submit" to them as spiritual leaders among them (Heb. 13:17).

Elders' role as "pastors" fits the metaphor of the church as a flock of sheep. Lambs and sheep must be fed, cared for, and protected. This calls for men versed in the "apostles' doctrine" or "sound doctrine," which enables them to teach, exhort, or convict gainsayers (Acts 2:42; Tit. 1:9). Many wolves in sheep's clothing seek to devour the flock, and pastors must, as did Jesus, willingly lay down their lives for the sheep (see John 10:7-15).

Deacons

Deacon is the English spelling of the Greek word *diakonos*. Of the 29 or 30 occasions the term is used in the New Testament, it is translated "deacon" only three times (Phil. 1:1; 1 Tim. 3:8,12). At other places it is rendered either "minister" or "servant." Deacons are servants in the local church and are under the oversight of the elders. Their role is to serve the needs of the local church. What might those needs be? They are not specifically enumerated in Scripture.

Some scholars see the seven men who served widows in the church at Jerusalem as examples for deacons (Acts 6:1-6). Grecian widows had physical needs that were not being supplied. They complained. Apostles could not leave the ministry of the word to "serve tables," a reference to the business of providing the widows' needs. "Serve" is a verb form of *diakonos* and suggests the type service deacons may render in the church. These and many other needs of a local church demand the appointment of capable, righteous, dedicated, and qualified "deacons" to minister (see 1 Tim. 3:8-13).

Evangelists/Teachers

Local churches consist of "saints in Christ Jesus. . .with the bishops and deacons" (Phil. 1:1). Among those saints may or may not be an evangelist, depending on the wisdom and discretion of the elders. Evangelists can be valuable assets to local churches, but are not essential to their completeness in Christ. Christ gave this gift to men for the perfecting of the saints and the building up of the body of Christ (Eph. 4:11,12). Timothy was left to work with the church at Ephesus and Titus with churches on the isle of Crete (1 Tim. 1:3; Tit. 1:5).

Timothy was specifically instructed to "do the work of an evangelist, fulfill thy ministry" (2 Tim. 4:5). Evangelist means "preacher" and is rooted in the New Testament words "gospel" and "preach." Evangelists are strictly charged to "preach the word; be urgent in season, out of season; reprove, rebuke, exhort, with all longsuffering and teaching" (2 Tim. 4:2). They are to charge brethren "not to teach a different doctrine, neither to give heed to fables and endless genealogies, which minister questions"; they are to insist that brethren consent to sound words and the doctrine of Christ which is according to godliness; they are equipped thoroughly and completely by the inspired message to teach, reprove, correct, and instruct in righteousness (see 1 Tim. 1:3,4; 6:3; 2 Tim. 3:16,17). The evangelist must work in the local church with the consent and under the oversight of the elders.

Teachers. Christians by reason of time and diligent study qualify themselves to teach others. Teachers were prominent in the church at Antioch and may have been among those who received the spiritual gifts of "wisdom" and "knowledge." Others were trained and taught by evangelists and were charged with the responsibility to instruct others (see Heb. 5:11-14; Acts 13:1; 1 Cor. 12:8; 2 Tim. 2:2).

Principles

A number of principles or conclusions grow out of New Testament teaching concerning congregational organization. First the negative.

> An "episcopal" form of church government in which a bishop rules a diocese of churches is both unscriptural and anti-scriptural. Bishops are overseers of a local church.

> A "presbytery" form of government in which a national assembly of elders meet annually to decide church policy for all local congregations has no Bible authority.

A "pope" who claims to be head or bishop of the church universal and asserts infallible authority over local churches is assuming a role given only to the Lord Jesus Christ.

A "mother" church which maintains control over a newly formed local church and oversees and rules the "infant" church finds no precedent in scriptural teaching or examples.

A number of positive conclusions follow from the biblical principles concerning the local nature of congregational structure.

Equal. All local congregations stand on equal ground before the Lord Jesus who is the head of the church. Not once does the New Testament portray a local church of higher standing or greater value than other local churches.

Independent. All local churches were independent of every other local church. The church in Antioch was not dependent upon the church in Jerusalem for authority. Each congregation stood before the Lord and bowed only to his authority when carrying out his work on earth.

Autonomous. The word "autonomous" means "self-rule" and denotes the responsibility of each church to control, decide, direct, and rule itself in harmony with the Lord's authority. No church determines for any other church its policies, its work program, its expediencies in worship, its benevolent work, or its program of edification.

Each local church has its own elders/bishops/pastors and must execute the Lord's will according to his commands in the best interest of what's scriptural and beneficial to the flock of God among them. No national headquarters or organization is authorized to dictate to equal, independent, autonomous local churches under the oversight of their own bishops.

Conclusion

The Jerusalem church was no exception to this. What happened at Jerusalem, according to Acts 15, is often proposed as an example of regional or national control of local churches by assemblies, conferences, or episcopal authority. Such a conclusion is an aberration and misunderstanding of the circumstances.

What happened at Jerusalem could happen anytime. Brethren from the Jerusalem church had gone out from that city to other churches, proclaiming false doctrine. Particularly, false brethren said to the church at Antioch — "Except ye be circumcised after the custom of Moses, ye cannot be saved" (Acts 15:1).

They had also taken this Mosaic tradition to the regions of Syria and Cilicia.

Paul and Barnabas, who earlier worked with the church at Antioch (Acts 13:1-3; 14:2-28), returned from their first preaching tour to find this problem. They came to Jerusalem to report their success among Gentiles and to confront the church about this teaching. The apostles and elders "with the whole church" acknowledged "that certain who went out from among us have troubled you with words, subverting your souls" (Acts 15:24). They wrote a letter containing this admission and named two from among them to travel with Paul and Barnabas to Antioch, Syria, and Cilicia with this message. This set the record straight with brethren whom their own members had offended.

The church at Jerusalem rejected what these false teachers taught, did not teach it at Jerusalem, and gave no commandment for them to teach it. It was no example of a national or regional assembly deciding truth or establishing ordinances for the church general. It was an instance of revelation at a time when Scripture was not complete (Acts 15:28). The letter was inspired as surely as the epistles to the Corinthians, Thessalonians, or Colossians — letters which were occasionally circulated to other churches (see Acts 15:28; Col. 4:16). It was particularly a letter from one church to others that had been subverted by its members.

When brethren recover the faith, love, and zeal of first-century Christians, the church will see no need to establish and support extra-congregational organizations to fulfill its mission. They will need no missionary societies or sponsoring elderships to map out and oversee their work of evangelism; no benevolent institutions to perform and supervise the care of their widows or other needy brethren; no Bible colleges to edify and perfect their saints. Each church can do all these things for themselves under the oversight of their own elders. God designed it that way and it's up to his church to respect and submit to it.

An Outline Study Guide

Introduction:

A. Describe the universal church and its organization. _____

_____

B. Why does a local church need elders to function efficiently? _____

_____

Elders:

A. Summarize the work of apostles and prophets (Eph. 3:1-6; 2:19-22). _____

_____

B. List three terms for elders (Acts 20:17,28; 1 Pet. 5:1-3). _____

What does each term emphasize? _____

C. Show that elders, bishops, and pastors describe the same office or function.

_____

_____

D. Discuss the jurisdiction of elders (Acts 14:23; 1 Pet. 5:1-3). _____

_____

E. Briefly analyze the qualifications of elders (1 Tim. 3:1-7; Tit. 1:5-9). ____

_____

Deacons:
A. Define the word "deacon" and tell how it originated. _____

_____

B. What gives some indication of the deacon's work (Acts 6:1-6)? _____

_____

C. List some possible services they might render today. _____

_____

Evangelists:
A. Who are two Bible examples of evangelists (1 Tim. 1:3; 2 Tim. 4:5; Tit. 1:5)? _____

_____

B. How do you know Timothy was an evangelist (2 Tim. 4:5)? _____

C. What does "evangelist" mean? Give the root word. _____

_____

D. Detail the work of an evangelist (2 Tim. 4:2,3). _____

_____

E. What equips him to be an evangelist and what is he enabled to do (2 Tim. 3:16,17)? _____

_____

F. What relationship does an evangelist have to elders? _____

_____

G. How are teachers qualified (Heb. 5:11-14; 2 Tim. 3:16,17)? What may they

have especially received in New Testament times (1 Cor. 12:8)? _____

_____

_____

H. How are evangelist related to teachers (2 Tim. 2:2)? _____

_____

Principles:
A. Outline some negative conclusions that grow out of this study. _____

_____

_____

B. Outline some positive conclusions from this study. _____

_____

_____

Conclusion:
A. Was Jerusalem national headquarters for the church (Acts 15)? _____ If

not, why?   Explain their relationship to Antioch, Syria, and Cilicia on the

matter of circumcision. _____

_____

B. When brethren take seriously congregational organization what kinds of

arrangements are eliminated? _____

_____

Mission:
Pillar And Ground of the Truth

Introduction

In 1896 Charles Sheldon, a Congregational minister, wrote a sentimental, idealistic novel entitled *In His Steps*. The book was subtitled, "What Would Jesus Do?" The novel explores the problems of modern society through the lives of the members of a "typical" American Protestant Church. The author highlights his answers to how Jesus would handle ills that had infected a newly industrialized America. The story reaches its climax when two preachers abandon their pulpits to establish a settlement house in a Chicago slum to help jobless, homeless, beleaguered citizens, and, in general, to "redeem" the community of its social, economic, moral, and political ailments. Sheldon's work is dominated by the view that the church's mission is to create a better world here and now — *on earth*!

In His Steps is clearly a product of its times and reflects what had become a growing American Protestant opinion at the opening of the twentieth century. Protestant preachers one by one had given themselves to what is now called by historians "The Social Gospel Movement." Sheldon, along with Washington Gladden, Josiah Strong, Shailer Mathews, Francis Peabody, Walter Rauschenbusch, Charles Foster Kent, and others, championed "social redemption" — belief that God's kingdom is a perfect, utopian social order in this world.

Sheldon's work is "fiction" in more ways than one. It never once raises the question — Who is Jesus? Passing directly to "What would Jesus do?" the author ignores the basic issue that Jesus is "God in the flesh" and that as Deity he humbled himself as a servant of God to make atonement for sin (Phil. 2:5-8); that he was named "Jesus" because he would "save his people from their sins" (Matt. 1:21); that he came to purchase with his blood a spiritual kingdom (Rev. 5:9,10). *In His Steps* totally distorts the work and role of Jesus among men. The "social gospel" takes root in theological liberalism — a modernistic concept that denies the transcendence of God, the deity of Jesus, the verbal inspiration of the Bible, and the immortal nature of man's spirit. These fundamental distortions blind social gospelers to the biblically revealed mission of the church.

Remnants of the social gospel, unfortunately, have entered most conservative Protestant bodies. Churches today, which claim to believe the Bible, lend their support to choreographed worship that competes with TV and movies, country club atmospheres that appeal to athletes and social bugs, medical clinics that transmit wrong signals about man's real worth, and soup lines that attract the poor who have little interest beyond the need of an empty stomach. Does any of this find support in the teaching of Scripture? What was the mission of the first-century church?

Evangelism

The biblical answer to these questions begins with the understanding of man's nature: that he is more than a body (Jas. 2:26); that he has a spirit made in the image of God (Gen. 1:26); that this spirit is eternal (Matt. 10:28); that man cannot live by bread alone but by God's word (Matt. 4:4); that "all have sinned, and fall short of the glory of God" (Rom. 3:23); that the wages of sin is the second death in a lake of fire and brimstone (Rom. 6:23; Rev. 21:8). "There is none righteous, no, not one" and all are doomed to spiritual ruin (Rom. 3:10).

In response to this spiritual problem the Lord was born and was named "Jesus" — "for it is he that shall save his people from their sins" (Matt. 1:21). After recording Jesus' success in bringing Zacchaeus to repentance and salvation from sins, Luke explained the Lord's mission: "For the Son of man came to seek and save that which was lost" (Luke 19:10). So wrote Paul: "Christ Jesus came into the world to save sinners; of whom I am chief" (1 Tim. 1:15). One would reasonably expect that the goal of the church is but an extension of the Lord's own mission. And that is precisely what Scripture teaches.

The preparatory work of Jesus in his public ministry culminated in his issuance of the Great Commission just before his ascension. To the immediate disciples he said, "Go ye into all the world, and preach the gospel to the whole creation" (Mark 16:15); "make disciples of all the nations" (Matt. 28:19); "repentance and remission of sins should be preached. . .unto all the nations" (Matt. 28:19; Luke 24:47). Behind this commission is "all authority," which Jesus received in heaven and on earth (Matt. 28:18). The Lord who came to save sinners authorized this work.

Paul defined the gospel: "Now I make known unto you, brethren, the gospel which I preached unto you, which also ye received, wherein also ye stand, by which also ye are saved, if ye hold fast the word which I preached unto you, except ye believed in vain. For I delivered unto you first of all that which also I received: that Christ died for our sins according to the scriptures; and that he was buried; and that he hath been raised on the third day according to the scriptures" (1 Cor. 15:1-4). The gospel declared Jesus' death "for our sins" and that is the message of the Lord's commission.

Paul preached this gospel at Corinth where he proclaimed "that Jesus was the

Christ" and "many of the Corinthians hearing believed, and were baptized" (Acts 18:5,8). Note the absence in either the commission or Paul's preaching of any "social," "political," "economic," or "entertainment" message. The mission of each generation of disciples, according to the Lord's order, is to teach them "to observe all things whatsoever I commanded you. . .even to the end of the world" (Matt. 28:20).

The church, as the book of Acts details, grasped fully this mission and performed it. The book opens the day Jesus ascended. He reminded the disciples of their work: "But ye shall receive power, when the Holy Spirit is come upon you: and ye shall be my witnesses both in Jerusalem, and in all Judea and Samaria, and unto the uttermost part of the earth" (Acts 1:8). That task began ten days later at the Jewish feast of Pentecost. That day Jesus was preached as Lord to the Jews and many were convicted of sins and responded obediently to the command: "Repent ye, and be baptized every one of you in the name of Jesus Christ unto the remission of sins" (Acts 2:36-41).

The apostles surrendered themselves wholly to the ministry of "the word of God" and taught the disciples that mission. When persecution arose in Jerusalem and the disciples were scattered throughout the regions of Judea and Samaria, "they. . .went about preaching the word" (see Acts 6:2; Acts 8:4). A few traveled as far north as Antioch of Syria to establish churches. The church in Antioch sent Paul, Barnabas, Silas, and others into other parts of the world with this message (see Acts 11:19-26; 13:1-3). Churches that Paul established supported him in his travels to preach. Churches were taught to provide "carnal things" (wages) to preachers who give themselves to "spiritual things" (the gospel) (see Phil. 4:15,16; 2 Cor. 11:8; 1 Cor. 9:11). The church saw itself as "the pillar and ground of the truth" and fulfilled that role by upholding, supporting, and proclaiming the word of God (see 1 Tim. 3:15).

Edification

Support of the truth also demanded that the church edify or build up its own members in the faith. Baptized believers were taught the need to maintain faithfulness unto Christ as Lord. Brethren at Jerusalem "continued stedfastly in the apostles' doctrine and fellowship, in the breaking of bread and the prayers" (Acts 2:42). Steadfastness calls for knowledge, increased faith, spiritual strength, and whole-hearted commitment. These come by what the Bible calls — "edification."

"Edification" means "to build up" and denotes the church's responsibility for growth "unto the building of itself in love" (Eph. 4:16). The Ephesian letter lists gifts Jesus gave to men for this purpose: "And he gave some to be apostles; and some, prophets; and some, evangelists; and some, pastors and teachers" (Eph. 4:11). The gifts were designed "for the perfecting of the saints, unto the work of ministry, unto the building up of the body of Christ" (Eph. 4:12).

Apostles and prophets laid the foundation of the church by the revelation of the gospel (see Eph. 2:20-22; 3:1-5). Evangelists, pastors, and teachers by this avenue of revelation perfected the saints. "Perfect" means to "equip," as in fishermen "*mending* their nets" (Matt. 4:21). "Mending" comes from the same family of words as "perfecting" and means to equip or prepare nets to do what nets are supposed to do. So the church must equip or prepare saints to do what saints are supposed to do.

Saints are designed to do "the work of ministry" — the work of service in the kingdom. Greatness in God's kingdom is based on service or ministry, not position or authority (see Matt. 20:20-28). Ministry includes preaching the gospel, teaching the brethren, restoring the erring, bearing burdens for the distressed, helping the needy, cheering the fainthearted, admonishing the disorderly, comforting the brokenhearted (see Acts 8:1-3; 2 Tim. 2:2; Gal. 6:1,2; Acts 4:32-35; 1 Thess. 5:14; 2 Thess. 3:15; 1 Thess. 4:17). The church must be equipped for these tasks.

The church also works toward the "building up of the body of Christ" or the "building up itself in love" (Eph. 4:12,16). It strengthens itself so that all members might arrive at a oneness of the faith, attain unto the knowledge of Christ, and measure up to the stature of the fullness of Jesus. When maturity develops, members are "no longer children, tossed to and fro and carried about with every wind of doctrine, by the sleight of men, in craftiness, after wiles of error" (Eph. 4:13,14). The church that edifies itself with a teaching program seeks to protect the body and each member from false teachers who by Satan's influence seek to devour (see 1 Pet. 5:8).

Edification is the reason brethren assemble. They "consider one another to provoke unto love and good works; not forsaking our own assembling together as the custom of some is, but exhorting one another" (Heb. 10:24,25). Several times Paul used some form of the word "edify" to teach the Corinthian brethren the purpose of the assembly (1 Cor. 14:3,4,5,17,26). "What is it then, brethren? When ye come together, each one hath a psalm, hath a teaching, hath a revelation, hath a tongue, hath an interpretation. *Let all things be done unto edifying*" (1 Cor. 14:26).

The same gospel that draws man to Christ and to salvation increases knowledge, builds faith, enhances love, and strengthens hope. This work is an extension of the church's responsibility as the "pillar and ground of the truth" (1 Tim. 3:15).

Benevolence

The church at the outset responded to brethren who were bereft of physical necessities. A bit of mystery surrounds the circumstances creating the need, and yet some brethren in the infant church could not provide their material needs. Brethren sold possessions and in other ways accumulated funds that were laid at the apostles' feet. Luke reveals the generous spirit that prevailed among them:

> And the multitude of them that believed were of one heart and soul: and not one of them said that aught of the things which he possessed was his own; but they had all things common. . .For neither was there among them any that lacked: for as many as were possessors of lands or houses sold them, and brought the prices of the things that were sold, and laid them at the apostles' feet: and distribution was made unto each, according as any had need (Acts 4:32,34,35).

"Benevolence" meant originally "to wish well" and now describes in English — acts of kindness, charitableness, doing good for needy ones. The New Testament does not use the word, but the term accurately describes what the newly born saints did for one another. Later Grecian widows were neglected in a daily distribution and complained to the church. The apostles implemented a method of seeing that no one's needs were unmet. Seven men were selected and appointed to "serve tables," an expression denoting allocation of goods to the poor (see Acts 6:1-6).

Hard times befell brethren on other occasions. Famine hit Judea a decade or so later and brethren in Antioch sent relief to the hands of the elders for disbursement among the indigent saints (see Acts 11:27-30). Much later saints in Jerusalem suffered a similar fate and Paul urged churches of Macedonia, Galatia, and Achaia to contribute on the first day of the week into treasuries that could be taken to the "poor saints" (see 1 Cor. 16:1,2; 2 Cor. 8,9; Rom. 15:22-29).

The silence of Scripture about general benevolence in communities has provoked serious discussion and many public debates. Christians are instructed to "visit the fatherless and the widows in their affliction" and "to do good unto all men," but the church as a body was never authorized to alleviate world poverty. Is such a view selfish and self-centered? Some say yes, but other conclusions are possible. The Lord in his wisdom may have spared the church from an impossible task and from being sidetracked into work that would distort its purpose on earth and detract from its essential mission to save souls.

The Bible sharply distinguishes between what individual Christians may do and what the church is to do. Paul wrote to Timothy about the obligation of relatives to provide for their own and "let not the church be burdened" (1 Tim. 5:16). He taught that "one member" may have roles that the "body" itself does not have, for "the body is not one member, but many" (1 Cor. 12:14). Many distortions of the church's mission manifest themselves when a distinction is not maintained between the "church" and the "individual."

● Paul was a tentmaker, as were Aquila and Priscilla, but that does not authorize the church to enter this or any other business (Acts 18:1-4).

● Parents were responsible for the training, education, and rearing of their children, but that does not authorize the church to get into the business of secular education (Eph. 6:1-4).

● Christians owned houses and land, but that does not authorize the church to own apartments, farms, and real estate for material gain (Acts 16:15,34).

● Disciples were responsible, as the good Samaritan illustrates and as opportunity and ability allow, to minister to the needs of strangers who have been victimized, but that does not authorize the church to build inns, motels, and half-way houses (Luke 10:25-37).

Conclusion

The New Testament is the sole source from which the church can learn its mission in the world. Ancient brethren under the direction of the apostles provide no example or precedent for the church to sponsor social events, supply entertainment, attack world poverty, agitate political upheaval in the name of Christ. The Lord and his apostles taught the church to evangelize the world, edify the disciples, and meet the physical needs of the brethren. The church gave itself wholly and fully to those tasks and in just 30 years reached the ends of the known world with the gospel and developed into a spiritually powerful body of believers that forever influenced the world (see Col. 1:23). Their zeal and dedication are to this day admired and praised by all who read the stirring story of their success. May the church today first give themselves to the Lord and seek to recapture that commitment and enthusiasm without modifying the goals the Lord set before it (see 2 Cor. 8:5).

An Outline Study Guide

Introduction:

A. Discuss Sheldon's book. What was its main message? _____

_____

B. What question did Sheldon ignore? _____

What is its importance? _____

C. List some remnants of "social gospel" among conservative Protestants. ___

_____

Evangelism:

A. Explore the nature of man (Gen. 1:26; Matt. 10:28). _____

_____

B. Why was Jesus born (Matt. 1:21)? _____

Why did he come into the world (1 Tim. 1:15)? _____

C. Summarize the "Great Commission" (Matt. 28:18-20; Mark 16:15,16; Luke 24:47). _____

_____

D. How did Paul define the gospel (1 Cor. 15:1-3)? _____

_____

What did he preach at Corinth (Acts 18:5,8; 1 Cor. 2:2)? _____

E. What do you learn from Acts about evangelism (Acts 1:8; 8:1-4; 11:19-26; 13:1-3)? _____

_____

F. Discuss the church's financial responsibility to those who preach the gospel (Phil. 4:15,16; 2 Cor. 11:8; 1 Cor. 9:11). _____

_____

Edification:

A. Describe the lives of the Jerusalem saints after baptism (Acts 2:42). _____

_____

B. Define "edification." _____

What gifts were given to effect edification (Eph. 4:11)? _____

_____

C. What does "perfecting" the saints mean? _____

D. What determines greatness in the kingdom (Matt. 20:20-28)? _____

_____ What duties does service include? _____

_____

E. Why must the church edify itself (Eph. 4:13,14; 1 Pet. 5:8)? _____

_____

F. Discuss edification and the assembly (1 Cor. 14:3,4,5,17,26)._____

_____

Benevolence:
A. Describe the inspiring example of benevolence at Jerusalem (Acts 4:32-35).

_____

    Who had a complaint and how was it handled (Acts 6:1-6)? _____

B. How did churches react to other churches which had need (Acts 11:27-30; 1 Cor. 16:1-3)? _____

_____

C. Are there examples of general benevolence by the church? _____
    What is a possible explanation for this? _____

D. Discuss the difference between the "church" and "individuals" (1 Tim. 5:16; 1 Cor. 12:12-14). _____

_____

    Detail examples of differences. _____

_____

Conclusion:
A. What is conspicuous by its absence in the work of the church? _____

_____

B. How successful was the church in its mission (Col. 1:23)? _____
C. What will it take for success today (2 Cor. 8:5)? _____

_____

Worship:
In Spirit and Truth

Introduction

Worship is universal among men. Has not man always bowed before some object, person, or cause that he esteemed greater than himself? It may have been the God of the universe, a silver or gold shrine, a noble and sacrificial humanitarian, or a movement committed to the advancement of mankind. To the worshipper, in harmony with the original meaning of the English word "worship," it was an object of value or worth to which he gave honor and allegiance; it became his ultimate concern. Man, on his own and without guidance, has been known to devote himself reverently to an almost endless number and variety of gods.

But is man on his own? Is he without guidance? Are there any directions for true worship? Or, must man decide this for himself? These are questions that God himself has answered by his Son. He approved of Jesus as God in the flesh by signs and wonders and bore witness: "This is my beloved Son, in whom I am well pleased, *hear ye him*" (John 1:1,14; Acts 2:22; Matt. 17:5). And his Son has spoken to man about worship. He said in a discussion with a Samaritan woman:

> But the hour cometh, and now is, when the true worshippers shall worship the Father in spirit and truth: for such doth the Father seek to be his worshippers. God is a Spirit: and they that worship him must worship in spirit and truth (John 4:23,24).

Jesus was specific about true worship: that it must be directed to "God" the Father; that it must be offered in "spirit"; and that it must be according to "truth." Worship is not just anything man decides, but what the Lord himself authorizes.

Man has always learned this lesson with difficulty. He has traditionally erred in the three ways Jesus specified. Israel stumbled again and again when by the influence of paganistic worship their reverence turned from God to idols. Most all worshippers have at times offered Jehovah a heartless, spiritless ritual of meaningless observances. And others have assumed that worship is worship, that sincerity is the litmus test, and that specific services need not be authorized by God. What, then, is Jesus telling us about true worship?

God
First, the object of man's worship must be God. Satan even tried to lure Jesus into violation of this sacred truth. Tempting Jesus to worship him in exchange for world power, Satan promised him: "All these things will I give thee, if thou wilt fall down and worship me" (Matt. 4:9). Jesus' answer sets before true worshippers the one object of worship: "Thou shalt worship the Lord thy God, and him only shalt thou serve" (Matt. 4:10). The simple reason for this: "I am Jehovah, and there is none else; besides me there is no God" (Isa. 45:5). "There is. . .one God and Father of all who is over all, and through all, and in all" (Eph. 4:6).

Cornelius, the first Gentile convert, learned this important lesson regarding man himself. When the apostle Peter came to him in answer to an angelic vision, the grateful, devoted, and humble Gentile "fell down at his feet, and worshipped him." Peter lifted him to his feet and said: "Stand up; I myself also am a man" (Acts 10:25,26). Even an apostle was taught this valuable lesson about angels. Two times John fell in worship before the angel who sent him the visions of Revelation and both times the angel represented himself as a fellow-servant and said succinctly: "Worship God" (Rev. 19:10; 22:9). No man, object of nature, humanitarian cause, earthly pursuit, or even an angel is worthy of worship.

Spirit
Worship of God must also be "in spirit." But what is the "spirit" of worship? The answer is found in the very nature of man. God is a Spirit and man is made in his image (see John 4:24; Gen. 1:26). Spirits do not have flesh and bones, so the likeness of man to God is not the body (see Lk. 24:39). Man, in addition to the body, has an inward man — a spirit or soul that identifies him with the likeness of God (see Matt. 10:28; Jas. 2:26).

Man's worship of God in spirit arises as an expression of the inward man (see 2 Cor. 4:16; Eph. 3:16). The spirit of worship is described by the words translated "worship" in the New Testament. *Sebō* or *sebomai* means "to revere" and denotes piety, godliness, and devoutness. They describe awe and adoration that fill the soul of man who genuinely worships God. *Proskuneō* or *proskunētēs* literally says "to kiss the hand to (towards) one, in token of reverence" as a spirit-filled expression of honor and devotion and obeisance (John 4:23,24). *Latreuō*, "to serve" or "to render religious service," is to be a "spiritual" or "reasonable" service — one that springs up from the mind or heart of man (Rom. 12:1).

Trees, animals, stars, the sun, the earth — all creation serves God's will and displays his handiwork and design. But only man, of all earthly creation, can offer heartfelt, spiritual worship and service to God. Man's unique likeness to God enables him and God requires him to: love God with all his *heart* and soul and mind; obey from the *heart* that form of doctrine; sing and make melody in the *heart*; give as purposed in the *heart*; pray out of the *heart's* desire; discern in the *heart* the body and blood of Jesus; exercise the *mind* to discern good from evil; etc. (see Matt. 22:37; Rom. 6:17; Eph. 5:19; 2 Cor. 9:7; Rom. 10:1; 1 Cor. 11:26; Heb. 5:13,14).

Jesus stressed this in strong indictments of Pharisaic hypocrisy. They prayed, gave alms, and fasted with great fanfare — merely to be seen of men (Matt. 6:1-18; see 23:13-36). Jesus rebuked their absent-minded, ritualistic worship and service in unmistakeable words. "This people honoreth me with their lips; but their heart is far from me" (Matt. 15:8).

Man is the crowning glory of God's earthly creation and with that comes responsibility. Man must not act robotically or instinctively. He is crafted distinctly by God as a rational, spiritual entity to respond to God's will out of reverence for God's person. Man is expected to know God, extol his worth, and worship him from the heart. From the depth of his soul, out of the sanctuary of a holy spirit, man is to "offer service well-pleasing to God with reverence and awe" (Heb. 12:28).

Truth

"Truth" is the third quality of true worship. The word "truth" often denotes the revealed gospel — as in "the word of truth" (Eph. 1:13; see 1 Thess. 2:13). When Jesus prayed to God he identified "thy word" as truth (John 17:17). "Love of the truth" is contrasted to what is a "lie" or "error" (2 Thess. 2:10-12). "Truth" says that worship must be based on God's word. Man does not decide out of his own wisdom how or in what manner he will worship God. Cain and Abel demonstrate this fact. They both worshipped God and brought offerings to God. Yet only Abel's sacrifice was accepted. The difference? "By faith Abel offered unto God a more excellent sacrifice than Cain, through which he had witness borne to him that he was righteous, God bearing witness in respect of his gifts" (Heb. 11:4). Faith made the difference because "faith comes by hearing, and hearing by the word of God" (Rom. 10:17). Abel's sacrifice was authorized by God. The same was true of Israel. Their worship and tabernacle services were revealed to Moses by God and constituted "divine services" (Heb. 9:1). Those who rejected it were punished (Lev. 10:1,2; 16:12; 2 Chron. 26:16-23).

Worship that is not based on truth is "vain." When Pharisees worshipped according to human traditions rather than God's word, Jesus said, "But in vain do they worship me, Teaching as their doctrines the precepts of men" (Matt.

15:9). Paul called the ascetic practices of philosophers who followed the rudiments of the world and traditions of men "will worship" — a "voluntary, arbitrary worship. . .which one devises and prescribes for himself" (Col. 2:8,23; see Thayer). The worship of the Athenians was ignorant worship and had to be corrected by apostolic revelation (Acts 17:23). Even "divine services" authorized by God for Israel are unacceptable for Christians under the new covenant (see Heb. 9:1; Gal. 4:8-11; 5:1-4).

They who worship God "must worship him in. . .truth." What is true of life in general is also true of worship: "O Jehovah, I know that the way of man is not in himself; it is not in man that walketh to direct his own steps" (Jer. 10:23). "There is a way which seemeth right unto a man; But the end thereof are the ways of death" (Prov. 14:12). God's will for the worship of the church can be discerned only from New Testament revelation.

Church

Assembly. The Lord's plan for worship by the church called for an assembly of the saints, an idea inherent in the word "church" itself. Paul wrote in considerable detail to the Corinthians about the assembly. The brethren had "come together in the church" to eat the Lord's supper. They had "come together not for the better but for the worse" by displaying a carnal, sectarian spirit and by transforming the supper into a common meal. That their "coming together be not unto judgment" the apostle instructed them in the proper observance of the memorial feast (1 Cor. 11:17-34).

Paul continued his discussion of the assembly in chapter 14 (see vv. 19,23,26,28,34,35), detailing and regulating the use of spiritual gifts. Whether singing, praying, or teaching, the goal of the assembly was "edification, and exhortation, and consolation" of the church. Brethren are ordered to "consider one another to provoke unto love and good works; *not forsaking our own assembling together*, as the custom of some is, but exhorting one another" (Heb. 10:24,25). Assembling for worship is a must for the church.

First Day. The first day of the week was particularly important to first-century Christians. Even historians a century or so later spoke of the assembly of the church upon the first day of the week (Justin Martyr). At Troas they came together "upon the first day of the week" to break bread and at Corinth brethren were commanded to contribute upon the first day of the week (Acts 20:7; 1 Cor. 16:1,2). That day was special to Christians, who served a Christ that was resurrected from death on that day (Luke 24:1-6). It was a specific day they assembled to offer prescribed acts of worship.

Lord's Supper. Sharing in the Lord's supper on the first day of the week was in memory of Christ's death. Jesus himself instituted the feast when he took unleavened bread to represent his body, gave thanks, broke the bread, and commanded the disciples to eat it in remembrance of him. He also took fruit of the vine, a likeness of his blood, gave thanks, and distributed it among them to drink in remembrance of him (Matt. 26:26-28; 1 Cor. 11:23-25).

The supper was not designed to transubstantiate the bread and fruit of the vine into the actual body and blood of Christ and to reoffer him as an "unbloody" sacrifice for mankind. This is the Catholic mass, not the Lord's supper. The supper was a memorial meal in which disciples remembered discerningly the Lord's body and proclaimed his death. Failure to do so was to eat and drink unworthily and bring damnation to the soul (1 Cor. 11:23-29).

Giving. The mission of the church demanded that brethren give. They gave upon the first day of the week to supply the physical needs of saints, furnish material support for men who preached the gospel, provide needed requirements for assembling, and meet any financial obligations that relate to the fulfillment of God's commands. The only command given to meet these needs is free-will offerings from the brethren. At Jerusalem early on brethren laid money at the apostles' feet to care for needy saints. Later the church was instructed to give according to their prosperity on the first day of the week. No mention is made of tithing, rummage sales, business investments, bingo parties, picnics and carnivals, real estate holdings, etc. The brethren offered freely out of devotion to God.

Each disciple was to lay by in a treasury; to give as God prospered him; to contribute on the first day of the week; to offer what he had purposed in his heart; to donate willingly and cheerfully, not grudgingly; and to present his gift sacrificially and liberally. Giving reverently out of a heart of gratitude and a spirit of devotion demanded that each one first give himself to the Lord (see 1 Cor. 16:1,2; 2 Cor. 8:2-5; 9:6,7).

Sing. Singing was another authorized avenue of worship in the first-century church. It is mentioned in at least seven different verses (see Acts 16:15; Rom. 15:9; 1 Cor. 14:15; Eph. 5:19; Col. 3:16; Heb. 2:12; Jas. 5:13). Singing edified the church as is apparent in Paul's order to sing "with the spirit, and . . . with the understanding" when the church comes together (1 Cor. 14:15). Paul admonished the church at Ephesus to speak "one to another in psalms and hymns and spiritual songs, singing and making melody with your heart to the Lord" (Eph. 5:19). Singing was for the mutual benefit of the church — "speaking to one another." It was patterned after the religious and devotional nature of "psalms," including "hymns" of praise and adoration to God, and, to avoid the secular and carnal, was characterized by "spiritual songs."

Finally, singing was to compose a "melody" in the heart. The phrase "making melody" comes from a Greek word that centuries before denoted pulling the hair, snapping a carpenter's plumbline, and plucking the strings of a harp. In New Testament times it described singing and, as here, the making of music in the heart. The apostle identified the heart as the instrument of spiritual praise and worship. Mechanical instruments are not prescribed by apostolic revelation, were unknown to the worship of the first century church, and are an act of will-worship devised by men. Only in modern times has their use become a general practice in denominational bodies.

Prayer. Paul also mentioned praying "with the spirit, and. . .with the understanding" in the assembly (1 Cor. 14:15). The Jerusalem church at the beginning "continued stedfastly in. . . prayers" (Acts 2:42). Christians learn both from the life of Christ and the apostle Paul how vital prayer is to their lives and work. Luke's gospel not only details the Lord's personal dedication to prayer (Luke 3:21; 5:16; 6:12; 9:18,28,29; 11:1; 22:41), but reveals his instruction to the disciples on how to pray and records his parable that teaches them they ought always to pray and not to faint (see Luke 11:1ff; 18:1ff). Most of Paul's epistles begin with descriptions of his prayers for the brethren or individuals to whom he writes and his requests for them to keep him in their prayers (Eph. 1:15-18; Phil. 1:3-7; Col. 1:3-12; 1 Thess. 1:2,3; Philem. 1:4-7).

Prayer was directed to God, who alone can send grace to help in time of need (see Rom. 10:1; Heb. 4:14-16). It included supplication, an appeal to God for needs; thanksgiving, an expression of gratitude for blessings received; intercession or petitions on behalf of others, whether enemies, brethren, kings, or one who had some special need of God's blessings (see 1 Tim. 2:1,2; Phil. 4:5,6). Prayer must be offered in faith, according to God's will, and in the name or authority of Christ (see Jas. 1:5-8; 1 John 5:14,15; John 14:13,14).

Teaching. The strength of brethren for life amidst an ungodly world came by the power of God's word to perfect, to train, and to edify. Brethren who were "without experience in the word of righteousness" were babes in Christ. Many by reason of time ought to have been teachers but needed to be taught again because they had not exercised and used their senses to discern good from evil (see Heb. 5:11-14). The word of God is "profitable for teaching, for reproof, for correction, for instruction which is in righteousness" (2 Tim. 3:16,17).

So when brethren assembled they received words of instruction, whether by tongues and their interpretation, by prophecy, by revelation, by teaching, by psalms (1 Cor. 14:19,26). When the brethren at Troas assembled to observe the Lord's supper, Paul discoursed to them until midnight. When Timothy preached at Ephesus, he was told to "preach the word. . .reprove, rebuke, exhort, with all longsuffering and doctrine" (2 Tim. 4:2). A vital part of the assembly service is the growth and development that comes by teaching.

Conclusion

The goal of this lesson is to look at the church, the assembly, and what brethren do as a body. Public worship cannot and must not take away from personal devotion to God daily. Man's praise of God and commitment to his word are qualities that reside permanently in the hearts of Christians and manifest themselves in the home, at work, in business dealing, over the backyard fence, or in an IRS office. Reverence for God colors and flavors all aspects of a Christian's life and is a constant power and influence over his behavior. Brethren who serve in "reverence and awe" sing, pray, meditate at all times (see Jas. 5:13; 1 Thess. 5:17; Psa. 1:2). Adoration for God is not just what Christians do — but what they are!

An Outline Study Guide

Introduction:

A. Discuss the universal nature of worship and detail various objects of worship.

_____

B. Summarize Jesus' outline of worship (John 4:24). _____

_____

C. How has man violated the principles of worship? _____

_____

God:

A. Describe Jesus encounter with "Satan worship" (Matt. 4:9,10). _____

_____

B. What did Cornelius learn about the object of worship (Acts 10:25,26)? ___

_____

C. Detail John's encounter with an angel (Rev. 19:10; 22:9). _____

_____

Spirit:

A. In what sense is man made in God's likeness (John 4:24; Gen. 1:26; Luke 24:39)? _____

_____

B. Analyze three words for worship. _____

_____

_____

C. Note the difference in man and other earthly creation. _____

_____

D. Man's worship proceeds from where? Give several examples. _____

_____

E. How did Jesus respond to Phariseeism (Matt. 6:1-18; 15:8; 23:13-36)? ___

_____

Truth:
A. What does truth describe (John 17:17; Eph. 1:13; 1 Thess. 2:13)? _____

_____

B. Show the difference between Cain and Abel's worship (Heb. 11:4). _____

_____

C. Give an example of:

   a. Vain worship: _____

   b. Will Worship: _____

   c. Ignorant Worship: _____

D. What does God say about man devising his own worship (Col. 2:8,23)? ___

_____

Church:
A. Justify an assembly for worship (Heb. 10:24,25; 1 Cor. 11:17-34). _____

_____

B. What day was important to the church (Acts 20:7; Luke 24:1-6)? _____

_____

C. List what brethren did in the assembly. _____

_____

D. Analyze all acts of devotion to God in the assembly:

   1. Lord's Supper: _____

   2. Giving: _____

   3. Singing: _____

   4. Praying: _____

   5. Teaching: _____

Conclusion:

A. Is worship limited to the assembly? If not, why? _____

_____

B. When should one sing (Jas. 5:13)? Pray? (1 Thess. 5:17)? Meditate (Psa. 1:2)? _____

_____

Discipline:
Purge out the Old Leaven

Introduction

Jehovah strictly ordered Israel not to join, blend, or mix things that are different (see Lev. 19:19; Deut. 22:9-11). He forbade them from yoking an ox and ass, weaving flax and wool into the same cloth, and sowing two kinds of seed in the same field. Why? A totally satisfactory answer is not known, but many agree that, in part, the law illustrated the need to keep the nation holy — separate from heathens and their profane practices.

Time and again, especially in Leviticus, God warned Israel against observing the "customs of the nation" which he had cast out of Canaan. Pagans had provoked Jehovah's anger and when their iniquity was full he "vomited" them out of the land (see Gen. 15:16; Lev. 20:22-26). Israel was to keep herself free from heathenism, lest she be driven from the land. God's message in Leviticus, after detailing the sacrifices, the consecration of the priesthood, and the laws of ceremonial cleansing, was: "Ye shall therefore be holy, for I am holy" (Lev. 11:14).

Cleansings of the flesh by offerings of bulls and goats were "types" of the spiritual purifying of the church by the offering of the blood of Christ (see Heb. 9:11-15; Eph. 5:25-27). The theme of Leviticus is repeated in the New Testament: "But like as he who called you is holy, be ye yourselves also holy in all manner of living; because it is written, Ye shall be holy; for I am holy" (1 Pet. 1:15,16). Paul stressed this truth when writing to brethren especially known for their unholy background and continued alliances with idolatry and immorality. "Be not unequally yoked with unbelievers" (2 Cor. 6:14).

Paul advanced this thought by a series of questions: "For what fellowship have righteousness and iniquity? Or what communion hath light with darkness? And what concord hath Christ with Belial? Or what portion hath a believer with an unbeliever? And what agreement hath a temple of God with idols?" (2 Cor. 6:14-16). He concluded: "Come ye out from among them, and be ye separate, saith the Lord, and touch no unclean thing" (2 Cor. 6:17).

"Unequally yoked" is one word in the original that combines two words: "different" and "yoke." The precise meaning is the tying or binding together of dissimilar things. This happens, according to his questions, when righteousness participates with iniquity, light shares with darkness, Christ blends his voice with Satan, believers are bound with unbelievers, or God's temple allies itself with idols. Unequal yokes result when Christians compromise with sin and partake in evil deeds.

The church must beware of this problem within its ranks. Impenitent brethren, factious men, immoral or disorderly disciples, and false teachers are not to be tolerated in the church. "Know ye not that a little leaven leaveneth the whole lump? Purge out the old leaven, that ye may be a new lump, even as ye are unleavened" (1 Cor. 5:6,7). Fellowship and company with unclean brethren will defile the whole church. The leaven of iniquity must be constantly purged if the purity of the church is to be maintained.

An Impenitent Brother

And if thy brother sin against thee, go, show him his fault between thee and him alone: if he hear thee, thou hast gained a brother. But if he hear thee not, take with thee one or two more, that at the mouth of two witnesses or three every word may be established. And if he refuse to hear them, tell it unto the church: and if he refuse to hear the church also, let him be unto thee as the Gentile and the publican (Matt. 18:15-17).

Jesus introduced the theme and procedure for dealing with impurity among brethren. He supposed that one brother sinned against another and then proposed the way to handle it. At first it is a private matter. The offended brother is to settle the matter personally. If the appeal to the sinful brother is heard and he corrects the injustice, the matter ends and he has gained a brother. But suppose the offending brother rejects the private rebuke?

The Lord said to take a couple of witnesses to establish before others the brother's sin and impenitence. After the offender's obstinacy is confirmed, the church needs to hear about it. The whole body of believers has responsibility and must be given opportunity to reach the erring brother with their appeals. Assuming that the church fails, the purging process, as the last resort, must begin.

"If he refuse to hear the church also, let him be unto thee as the Gentile and the publican." To an audience of Jews the Lord's sentence against the brother could not have been clearer. A wall of partition, the law of Moses, had totally separated Jews and Gentiles since the days of Moses. Absolutely no association was permitted between the two. Gentiles, Jews thought, were "dogs" — unclean and unfit for human acceptance (see Matt. 15:26). Publicans, even if Jews, were treated as Gentiles. As tax-collectors for Rome, whose rule Israel resented, they were rejected reprobates. To eat with publicans was to eat with sinners; to associate with them was to defile oneself.

Jesus' message is plain. Impenitent brethren are not worthy of company with faithful brethren and must be cut off absolutely. To let them "be unto thee as the Gentile and the publican" meant to ostracize them completely — not eat with them, fish with them, do business with them, ride in a chariot with them, welcome them into their homes. There may be no fellowship or company between righteousness and iniquity in the Lord's church.

An Immoral Brother

It is actually reported that there is fornication among you, and such fornication as is not even among the Gentiles, that one of you hath his father's wife. . .Put away that wicked man from among yourselves (1 Cor. 5:1,13).

The paganistic problem Moses warned Israel about in Leviticus plagued the church at Corinth. God in Moses' days foresaw idolatry and immorality becoming commonplace in the nation of Israel. Israel assured this result when they refused to drive heathens out of Canaan and later fraternized with them and accepted their worship. Idolatry inundated the land, the law was forgotten, and the "holy nation" succumbed to the grossest of immorality. Paul feared a similar outcome at Corinth.

Corinth, a Gentile city and seaport, was unequalled among most ancient cities for immorality. Their heathen religion hired 1000 prostitute priestesses with whom men honored the gods in sexual immorality. Fornication was common and raised few eyebrows. When Paul arrived in A. D. 51/52 he stood face to face with idolaters, thieves, adulterers, fornicators, homosexuals, murderers, drunkards, extortioners, and the like. Some, however, were touched by the gospel and became Christians (1 Cor. 6:9-11; Acts 18:8).

Inevitably some form of unrighteousness would make its way into the church. As Simon the sorcerer and a certain percentage of disciples, someone, like the hog and the dog, would fall away and return to wallowing in the mire and to eating the vomit of sin they left behind (see Acts 8:9-21; 2 Pet. 2:20-22). When it happened at Corinth it was worse than might be expected — a man was sexually immoral with his father's wife; a sin even Gentiles avoided (v. 1) Sadly, the brethren treated it as nothing, were "puffed up" about it, and did not even "mourn." What should have been done? He who did this deed should have been taken from among them (v. 2).

Paul stated his inspired judgment on the matter. The brethren by the authority of Christ should gather the entire church together and "deliver such a one unto Satan for the destruction of the flesh, that the spirit may be saved in the day of the Lord Jesus" (1 Cor. 5:3-5). In effort to save the brother God's family must reject him and turn him over to Satan and his evil cohorts. Leave him to his own kind in hopes that rejection by wholesome brethren will effect godly sorrow that conquers the flesh. To turn their heads and ignore such blatant sin among them was to encourage the practice generally. As "a little leaven leaveneth the whole lump," so a little sin will infect the whole body. "Purge out the old leaven" and "put away the wicked man from among yourselves" (1 Cor. 5:7,13).

Paul's point is "to have no company with" them, a word that means literally to "mix together," hence to "mingle" or "associate" with. He spoke of brethren, not fornicators or adulterers or thieves in the world. Cutting off all company with evil doers in the world would demand that Christians leave the world. Brethren are different. No relationship with immoral brethren may prevail until repentance is evident. This assures the purity of the church.

A Disorderly Brother

Now we command you, brethren, in the name of our Lord Jesus Christ, that ye withdraw yourselves from every brother that walketh disorderly, and not after the tradition which they received of us (2 Thess. 3:6).

The message to the church in Thessalonica parallels orders given to Corinth. Here the military term "disorderly" is introduced to describe an erring brother. The word suggests marching out of rank or out of step and denotes insubordinate behavior. Disorderliness is defined as violation of the traditions handed down by God and cannot be limited to the specific incident at Thessalonica. The case there was a brother who would "work not at all, but was a busybody" (v. 11). Refusing to provide for himself, he sponged off of other brethren and went about speaking concerning matters of private business.

Three things must be done. One, "note" this brother, a word that means to "mark" or put a "sign" on. It is used metaphorically and means to identify the brother openly — to publicly name him (v. 14). Two, have no company with him. "Company," meaning to "mix" or "mingle" or "associate," is the same word Paul used in the Corinthian epistle. All relationship with the brother must be severed (v. 14). Third, treat him not as an enemy but admonish him as a brother (v. 15). The apostle reminded the church that erring brethren are still brothers and are not to be objects of hate or evil doing. They are to be loved and every effort must be made to convert them from their error and restore them (see Gal. 6:1; Jas. 5:19,20).

A Factious Brother

Now I beseech you, brethren, mark them that are causing the divisions and occasions of stumbling, contrary to the doctrine which ye learned: and turn away from them. For they that are such serve not our Lord Jesus Christ, but their own belly; and by their smooth and fair speech they beguile the hearts of the innocent (Rom. 16:17,18).

The purity of the church is also threatened by factious men. As with the disorderly, factious men are to be marked. The word here means "to look at" or "behold" as though eyeing the man or drawing a bead on him; another way of saying the brother must be identified. These men cause divisions and occasions of stumbling among the brethren. They serve the flesh rather than Christ and deceive innocent brethren by flattering words. Their sin is threefold: They create division, cause brethren to stumble, and teach contrary to sound doctrine. From such the church is to "turn away" — veer off from their path. Refuse to walk with them.

Paul left Titus on the isle of Crete to set in order churches and warned him about divisive men. First, the evangelist must "shun foolish questionings, and genealogies, and strifes, and fightings about the law; for they are unprofitable and vain" (Tit. 3:9). Second, the preacher is to deal with "heretics" (KJV) or "factious men" (ASV). He is required to admonish them a "first" and "second" time (Tit. 3:10). After this he must "refuse" them; literally, "beg off" or excuse himself from them, as did the men who excused themselves and refused to attend a feast (see Lk. 14:18,19). Brethren who are, as Paul described them, "perverted" and "sinneth" and stand "self-condemned" cannot be accepted in the church, if it is to maintain its purity (Tit. 3:11).

A False Teacher

Paul named three despicable men who were a danger to the church in Ephesus. He, for that reason, left Timothy there to "charge certain men not to teach a different doctrine" (1 Tim. 1:3). Hymenaeus and Alexander had made shipwreck of the faith and endangered the faith of those who remained. Timothy is told to "fight the good warfare" and deliver these two men to Satan "that they might be taught not to blaspheme" (1 Tim. 1:20). False teachers, as immoral brethren, are to be rejected and left to have company only with those who serve the father of lies (see 1 Cor. 5:5; John 8:44).

Philetus was a part of a threesome at Ephesus. He and Hymanaeus had erred from the truth, contending that the resurrection was already past. The two had already overthrown the faith of some and had to be dealt with severely. Their word, if not stopped, would eat as doth gangrene and would poison the whole church (2 Tim. 2:16-18).

John, the apostle of love, faced and dealt harshly with false teachers toward the end of the century, when Gnosticism was making a strong move against the faith. He warned: "Whosoever goeth onward and abideth not in the teaching of Christ, hath not God" (2 John 9). Such men are not to be received into one's house and are not to be given greeting. Otherwise, brethren "partaketh in his evil works" (2 John 10). Receiving them into one's house was an act of hospitality extended to travelers, a form of support that helped them on their journey and sustained their work (see 3 John 5-8). The greeting of the day — "the grace and the peace of God be with you" — was likewise an endorsement of their work.

Conclusion

• A brother who is convicted of sin before witnesses and refuses to hear the truth and repent must be excluded totally from association with his brothers in Christ

• An immoral brother has violated his holy relationship with God and for the sake of his own salvation and the purity of the church is to be excluded from all company with God's sanctified sons and daughters.

• A disorderly brother is insubordinate to God's authority, having rejected his commandments and having refused to submit to his orders, and must not be permitted to march within the ranks of obedient soldiers of Christ

• A brother whose smooth speech and false doctrine beguiles brethren and causes division is perverted and unworthy to walk side by side with faithful brethren who have admonished and warned him. He must be openly rejected.

• A false teacher refuses to abide in and proclaim the teaching of Christ and is cut off from God and Christ. He may thus receive no greeting, support, or encouragement from the family of God. He is to be rejected and absolutely shunned by all who contend for the teaching of Christ.

An Outline Study Guide

Introduction:

A. What does the law say about mixing things that are different (Lev. 19:19; Deut. 22:9-11)? _____

B. How did this mixing apply to Israel as a nation? _____
_____

C. Discuss Old Testament cleansings as "types." What did God say to Israel that he says to Christians (Lev. 11:14; 1 Pet. 1:15,16)? _____
_____

D. What is said about "unequal yokes"? What is meant (2 Cor. 6:14-17)? ___
_____

E. How does this relate to the church (1 Cor. 5:6,7)? _____

_____

Impenitent Brother (Matt. 18:15-17):
A. Describe the hypothetical case Jesus raises. _____

_____

B. Outline the procedural steps of action. _____

_____

C. What does treat him as a Gentile or publican mean? _____

_____

Immoral Brother (1 Cor. 5):
A. Give background material on Corinth. What did Paul find there (1 Cor. 6:9-
    11)? _____

_____

B. Can brethren fall away (Acts 8:9-21; 2 Pet. 2:20-22)? _____
C. What sin plagued Corinth? _____
D. How had the church reacted to this brother? _____
E. Outline what Paul told the church to do. _____

_____

F. What conduct should Christians have toward fornicators of the world? ____

_____

Disorderly Brother (2 Thess. 3:6-15):
A. Define and discuss "disorderly." _____
B. What had the brother at Thessalonica done? _____
C. What three steps did Paul order? _____

_____

Factious Brother (Rom. 16:17,18; Tit. 3:9-11):
A. What is meant by "factious"? _____

B. What three things had the brethren at Rome done? _____

_____

C. How were brethren to respond to these men? _____

D. What two things is Titus instructed to do in Crete? _____

_____

E. How was Titus to deal with "heretics" or "factious men"? _____

_____

False Teacher (1 Tim. 18-20; 2 Tim. 2:16-18; 2 John 9-11):
A. What had Hymanaeus and Alexander done? _____

B. What is Timothy instructed to do? _____

_____

C. What were Hymanaeus and Philetus teaching? _____

D. What will false teaching among brethren do? _____

E. Who did John oppose? _____

F. What warning does he give? _____

G. How might brethren receive false teachers and partake in their evil

deeds? _____

Conclusion: Summarize and review each case of unfaithfulness. _____

_____

_____

Sufficiency:
The Secret Things Belong To God

Introduction

Sometime in the summer of 1809, according to one account, Thomas Campbell delivered a sermon in the house of Abraham Altars near Washington, Pennsylvania and concluded with these celebrated words:

> Where the Scriptures speak, we speak; and where the Scriptures are silent, we are silent (*Journey in Faith*, Lester G. McAllister and William E. Tucker 110).

Later that year Campbell wrote his renowned *Declaration and Address* in which the above words are not found, but the idea is expressed and expounded. Almost immediately, men who were determined to restore the "ancient order of things" adopted Campbell's words as a slogan. Accepting the slogan as a scriptural motto, Campbell and others believed it would direct men to the original ground of the first-century church, eliminate the "rubbish" of human traditions, and promote unity among men of diverse denominational backgrounds. To Campbell, the view demanded a "thus saith the Lord" for every religious practice and was a sure foundation for oneness in Christ.

The first part of Campbell's slogan met little resistance. Bible students, at least in principle, generally agree that man should speak as the Bible speaks. This, in fact, is precisely what the apostle Peter said: "If any man speak, let him speak as the oracles of God" (1 Pet. 4:11). But silence? That is another story. Sharp contention prevailed almost from the beginning over the meaning and application of this half of the slogan.

Silence to many is a signal for liberty, an indication that man may use his own judgment in deciding issues. Silence, they believe, "permits"; it allows the importation and application of human wisdom. Others strenuously argue that silence "forbids"; that "from nothing, nothing comes." If God says nothing, they contend, then nothing is authorized. Lack of Bible authority for religious practices prohibits those practices.

Biblical View of Silence

When, for example, God commanded men to be "baptized" (immersed,

Rom. 6:4; Acts 2:38) and said nothing about "sprinkling," does that forbid or permit sprinkling? Clearly, sprinkling is not authorized. But is it prohibited? Such issues are not raised to promote a special rule of biblical interpretation. It asks a question about communications in general. Does a father who sends his child to the store for potato chips need to specify each item the child is not to buy? Surely not! Does not the father's specific request exclude and forbid buying "snicker bars" or "chewing gum"? Does not the child who goes beyond his father's instructions introduce into the purchase — *his own will?* God's will, as man's, is expressed only by what he says — not by his silence. God says "baptism," not "sprinkling." To teach and practice sprinkling is speculative, presumptuous, and an injection of the human will into the divine scheme of redemption.

The Old Testament, written for Christians' learning and admonition (Rom. 15:4; 1 Cor. 10:11), illustrates the principle of silence. When Noah was commanded to build an ark, God said to build it out of "gopher wood" (Gen. 6:14). God uttered nothing about "oak," "maple," or "pine." Does not the nature of communications, in this case, eliminate woods other than gopher? If not, communication becomes impossible. Terms that mean anything a man wants them to mean may mean everything and speech becomes meaningless. Noah, according to such reasoning, could have said, "I understand gopher wood to mean and include crepe paper." To presume by God's silence that "oak" or "pine" or "maple" or "crepe paper" was acceptable would manifest Noah's own will — not God's!

The writer of Hebrews confirms the validity of this reasoning in an argument about the priesthood of Jesus (Heb. 7). Jesus, as the writer notes early in chapter seven, was a priest after the order of Melchizedek — not of Levi or Aaron. Jesus could not be a priest on earth under the law of Moses because he was from the wrong tribe — Judah. The writer's point is based on silence: "For it is evident that our Lord hath sprung out of Judah; as to which tribe Moses spake *nothing* concerning priests" (Heb. 7:14). Even Jesus could not presume on God's silence and include himself in the Mosaic priesthood.

Uzziah, king in Israel and of the tribe of Judah, learned this important truth. Presumptuously, the arrogant king entered the temple to burn incense. A company of priests approached the king and insisted: "It pertaineth not unto thee, Uzziah, to burn incense unto Jehovah, but to the priests the sons of Aaron, that are consecrated to burn incense" (2 Chron. 26:18). God had said *nothing* about descendants of Judah being priests. God's answer to the proud ruler's intrusion upon his silence was a plague of leprosy that broke out on Uzziah's forehead (2 Chron. 26:19-21).

Nadab and Abihu, sons of Aaron, also found out that God's silence forbids. Legitimate priests, the two entered the tabernacle to burn the incense. The law instructed them to take hot coals off the altar of sacrifice, put them in censers, take them into the tabernacle, put them on the altar of incense, and pour incense upon them (Lev. 16:11-14). But Nadab and Abihu used *"strange fire* before Jehovah, *which he had not commanded them"* (Lev. 10:1,2). The origin of the fire is not named, but it was a fire about which God had said nothing — "unauthorized fire," according to the NIV. God displayed his displeasure when he sent fire from heaven to devour the two priests.

Some may be skeptical of mere examples and prefer more direct statements of this truth. Consider, then, the words of Moses to Israel on the Plains of Moab before they entered Canaan. "Ye shall not add unto the word which I command you, neither shall ye diminish from it, that ye may keep the commandments of Jehovah your God which I command you" (Deut. 4:2). To speak where God had not spoken was to add human precepts to what had been divinely revealed, according to Moses. Jehovah plainly forbade Israel from adding to what he had said. One may argue or debate what is or is not an addition to God's words, but the principle of prohibitive silence is fundamental in God's revelation.

Moses in another place was even more emphatic. "The secret things belong unto Jehovah our God; but the things that are revealed belong unto us and to our children forever, *that we may do all the words of the law"* (Deut. 29:29). Two thoughts are prominent here. One, what God had not said was not for man to know. Wise and obedient men leave it at that. Two, what God said belonged to man and enabled him to "do all" that God expected of him. God's utterances furnish the man of God complete (2 Tim. 3:16,17). Man needs only what God has said and is limited to that. Thomas Campbell was right — where the Scriptures are silent, man must be silent.

What this study emphasizes and concludes is that the identity, nature, and character of the first-century church can be established only by what God has said. "Presumption" is the key word to describe the modern practice of speaking where God is silent and adding to the gospel. It arrogantly seeks to intrude into the sacred portals of the unfathomable mind of God. In reality it injects the human will, binds human traditions, divides so-called "Christendom," and brings condemnation. Speaking where the Bible speaks and remaining silent where the Bible is silent identifies a body of people in the twentieth century with the church Jesus built and distinguishes it from Catholicism and Protestant denominationalism. The church of Christ is identified by what God has spoken.

Review — Sufficiency and Identity

Membership. Paul was adamant about this when dealing with the problem of salvation from sin and membership in the church. Jesus in the "Great Commission" had revealed the mind of God concerning salvation. There the Lord taught men to believe, repent, and be baptized in order to be saved and to be added to the church (Matt. 28:18-20; Mark 16:15,16; Luke 24:47-49; 1 Cor. 12:13). The apostles proclaimed this message from the beginning at Pentecost and into every city where they took the gospel (see Acts 2:38; 8:12,13; 18:8; etc.). Paul had preached it at Galatia (Gal. 1:8). But *nothing* was said about circumcision being essential to salvation. No such commandment was given by the apostles or elders at Jerusalem (Acts 15:24).

And yet certain men came from Jerusalem to Antioch, other parts of Syria, and Cilicia with the message: "Except ye be circumcised after the custom of Moses, ye cannot be saved" (Acts 15:1). This practice was accepted by the churches of Galatia and Paul reacted firmly to the presumption. First, he said the brethren at Galatia had received a "different" gospel. Second, that it was not the same gospel he had preached and they had originally received. Third, that the preaching and acceptance of this different gospel would bring condemnation and sever them from Christ and his grace (see Gal. 1:6-9; 5:1-4). Men, according to Paul, must speak where God speaks and be silent where he is silent. The gospel as God revealed it and the church as Jesus built it are sufficient. "Whosoever goeth onward and abideth not in the teaching of Christ,hath not God" (2 John 9).

Foundation/Head. The foundation of the church is Christ — the tried, rejected, precious cornerstone. This foundation was laid by apostles and prophets to whom revelation of truth through the Holy Spirit was made known. The church is built on Christ and the truth of the gospel. Jesus was made the head of the church and the church is to be subject to him (1 Pet. 2:4-8; Eph. 2:19-22; 5:24). This eliminates Peter, human traditions, the pope, Catholic dogma, Protestant creeds, Martin Luther, and alleged modern revelations. Jesus Christ is a sufficient foundation and authority for the church today.

Name. The church belongs to Christ. He is its builder, ruler, and savior (Matt. 16:18; Eph. 1:22,23; 5:23-27). He was crucified for it and each member was baptized into his name (1 Cor. 1:10-13). Why then would brethren exalt other names? God, to honor Jesus, gave disciples the name "Christian" and instructed them to glorify him (God) in that name (Acts 11:26; 1 Pet. 4:16). Christians speak as God's oracles when they describe themselves as "churches of God" or "churches of Christ" (1 Cor. 1:2; Rom. 16:16). When they think of themselves as "Lutherans" or "Baptists" or "Presbyterians," they exalt men and sectarian viewpoints above Christ.

Organization. The churches of the first century knew nothing larger than local congregations. Each church, when men were qualified, appointed elders, who were known also as "bishops" and "pastors." Their work was to lead, rule, and oversee the church in which they were ordained. Each congregation was equal, independent, and autonomous. Elders had no oversight or control beyond the church in which they were selected (see Acts 14:23; 20:28; 1 Pet. 5:1-3).

Absent from their practice and from the Lord's instruction is anything remotely resembling a bureaucratic hierarchy of priests, bishops, archbishops, and a pope. No national assembly of presbyters, synod of bishops, or convention of representatives met to deliberate, analyze, and decide policy, doctrine, or procedures. Elderships did not sponsor and oversee works of evangelism, edification, or benevolence for other local churches. The church was sufficient in its local capacity to accomplish its mission in the world. Churches cooperated with other churches only when the receiving church was unable to meet its own need locally (see 2 Cor. 8:12-15).

Mission. The churches' mission was simple and basic. As the "pillar and ground of the truth," the church received a twofold mission: evangelism and edification (1 Tim. 3:15; Eph. 4:11-16). Churches proclaimed the gospel in their own communities and sent men to take the good news to other cities, supporting them directly without any intervening sponsoring churches (Acts 8:1-4; 13:1-3; 2 Cor. 11:8; Phil. 4:15,16). The church worked to perfect men and women who were baptized and to build them up to the measure of the stature of Christ. And when any among them was destitute, they took special care to provide for them the necessities of life (Acts 2:44,45; 4:32-35).

The country club atmosphere of modern churches was unknown. The building of kitchens, gymnasiums, video game rooms, athletic fields, "fellowship" or social halls may please the members and draw a crowd, but has no relationship to the gospel, the first-century church, and the salvation of souls. The gospel is God's power to save and is sufficient (Rom. 1:16). To attract men by "loaves and fish" is a secular appeal that is foreign to apostolic doctrine and practice (see John 6:26,27). The church Jesus built is identified by its confidence in and dependence on the gospel alone.

Worship. The assembly of the church and its worship is clearly identifiable (John 4:24). Brethren gathered together to remember Christ's death in the observance of the Lord's supper. They sang, prayed, studied, and gave as God had prospered them (Acts 20:7; 1 Cor. 11:23-26; 14:14,15; 16:1,2). All of this was done in simplicity to edify the church, not to entertain and stroke sensual pleasures.

Professionalism, whether of choirs or instrumental groups, were prominently absent from the first-century church. The clapping of hands, shouting, and confusion of many speaking at once were viewed as disorderly, a hindrance to edification, and a clear violation of God's will. Even before "tongues" ceased with the completion of New Testament revelation (see 1 Cor. 13:8-10), tongue speaking was unacceptable unless interpreted and practiced in turn — one at a time (1 Cor. 14:26-33,40).

Conclusion

Two or three impressions from this study must be apparent to the readers: one, the vast difference between the church Jesus built and the modern practices of Catholicism and Protestant denominations; two, the utter simplicity of the organization, work, and worship of the first-century church; three, the success of the New Testament church in meeting man's spiritual needs and accomplishing the work God designed for it.

Any body of obedient believers can identify with the church God designed and Jesus built when they eliminate the traditions of men, get "back to the Bible," and believe and practice what God spoke without addition, subtraction, and modification. May God bless all men with that conviction and commitment.

An Outline Study Guide

Introduction:
A. Recite Thomas Campbell's famous quotation. _____

_____

    What did Campbell think the slogan would accomplish? _____

_____

B. What part of the slogan created controversy? _____

C. Discuss two views of silence. _____

_____

Biblical View of Silence:
A. Illustrate silence with the father/child relationship. _____

_____

    How does this apply to sprinkling? _____

B. How can this be seen in God's command to Noah (Gen. 6:14)? _____

_____

C. Detail the Hebrew writer's argument from silence (Heb. 7:14). _____

_____

    Who in the Old Testament confirms this view (2 Chron. 26:16-21)? How?

_____

D. Explain the sin of Nadab and Abihu (Lev. 10:1,2; 16:11-14). _____

_____

E. What bearing do Deuteronomy 4:2 and 29:29 have on the argument from silence? _____

Review — Sufficiency and Identity:

A. Apply the principle of silence to membership in the church. _____

_____

B. Apply it to the foundation and headship of the church. _____

_____

C. Apply it to designations of the church. _____

_____

D. Apply it to the organization of the church. _____

_____

E. Apply it to the mission of the church. _____

_____

F. Apply it to the worship of the church. _____

_____

Conclusion:
A. Discuss three impressions from this study. _____

_____

_____

B. How can any body of obedient believers identify with Christ's church of the

first century? _____

_____